Femina Rajpal.

Karbala

The Complete Picture

Mahmood Husein Datoo

BSc PhD CEng MRAeS MIMechE MICE

e-mail: mahmood@datoo.org

Published by:
Tahrike Tarsile Qur'an, Inc.
Publishers & Distributors of The Holy Qur'an
80-08 51st Avenue
Elmhurst, New York 11373-4141
t: 718 446 6472 | f: 718 446 4370 | e: read@koranusa.org
www.koranusa.org

First US Edition 2011

ISBN: 978-1-879402-10-2
Library of Congress Control Number 2011920793

Regional Printers and Distributors:
European Hajj Mission, Council of European Jamaats (CoEJ)
22 Estreham Road, London, SW16 5PQ
www.eurohajjmission.org www.coej.org
e-mail: enquiries@eurohajjmission.org
First edition 3,000 copies

Organization of North American Shia Ithna-asheri Muslim Communities (NASIMCO)
CANADA: 300 John Street, PO Box 87629, Thornhill, ON, L3T 7R3
USA: PO Box 29691, Minneapolis, MN 55429
www.nasimco.org e-mail: info@nasimco.org
First edition 2,000 copies

Al-Itrah Foundation
P O Box 19701, Dar Es Salaam, Tanzania Tel: +255 22 2110640
www.alitrah.org e-mail: alitrah@raha.com
First edition 1,500 copies

Contents

Charts

The above ten charts are available in full size from www.mahmooddatoo.com

Abbreviations/Glossary

BH	Before Hijra (Islamic calendar)
AH	After Hijra (Islamic calendar) 1 AH corresponding to 622 AD
AD	Christian calendar
saww	Abbreviations in Arabic meaning “peace be on him and his household) - salutation following the name of the Prophet
as	Abbreviation in Arabic meaning “peace be on him/her” - salutation following the names of the members of the Prophet’s Household
Imam	Leader appointed by Allah (God)

Summary

The book starts by tracing the ancestors of Imam Husein (as) and Yazeed, the two principal figures involved in the tragedy of Karbala. The family tree of Imam Husein (as) is looked at in detail, with particular reference to those who are connected with the tragedy of Karbala.

The book then explores systematically the regional, political and religious developments during the time of the Holy Prophet and the succeeding leaders, Leader Abu Bakr, Leader Umar, Leader Othman and Imam Ali (as).

The circumstances leading to, and the content of, the political settlement between Imam Hasan (as) and Muawiya are explained. This is then followed by an account of the methods used by Muawiya to ensure his son Yazeed succeeds him as the leader of the Muslims.

The text then goes on to examine the situation when Yazeed comes to power. His demand for personal allegiance of Imam Husein (as) sparks off a chain of events that finally lead to the tragedy of Karbala. These events, from Madinah to Makkah to Kufa and finally to Karbala are elaborated upon step by step.

The activities of the days spent in Karbala are discussed and a full description is given of exactly what happened on the day of Ashura. The trials and tribulations experienced by the survivors of Karbala in Kufa and Damascus are outlined. Finally, the book ends with an analysis of who won the campaign and an overview of events that bring about the downfall of the Umayyas.

1 Family Tree

In this chapter, we will trace the ancestors of Imam Husein (as) and Yazeed, and look in some detail at the family tree of Imam Husein (as).

1.1 Ibraheem and Ismaeel

- We are looking at a time about four thousand years ago, when Prophet Ibraheem (as) is living in what is now Palestine; he has two wives - Sarah and Hajar; at that time, it was accepted to have more than one wife at a time.

- His first wife is Sarah and from this marriage, he has his second son called Ishaq. His second wife is Hajar and from this marriage, he has his first son called Ismaeel. Both his sons were also Prophets.

- Soon after the birth of Ismaeel, Allah commands Prophet Ibraheem (as) to take Hajar and baby Ismaeel to an area much further south; they take as much provisions of food and water as they can carry and set out southwards.

- Allah tells them to stop at an area where there are no other people around, and where there is no water supply and no vegetation.

- It is worth noting the absolute faith of Prophet Ibraheem (as) in Allah, by not questioning the command of Allah in this apparent motiveless emigration (from an area with comfortable amenities to an area with no amenities at all).

- Allah then commands Prophet Ibraheem (as) to leave Hajar and Ismaeel at this area, and for him to go back to his home.

- Hajar soon runs out of water from the provisions they carried; she leaves baby Ismaeel on the ground, and she runs between two nearby hills (Saffa and Marwa) in search of water, calling out for help.

- It was after her seventh run between the hills, that she sees a fountain of water miraculously springing up by the feet of the baby Ismaeel; this is the well of Zamzam which is springing water until today.

- When the birds in the sky see this oasis, they fly to this spot for water; travellers notice the flight of the birds, and they in turn also now come to the oasis as one of their stopping points; in time, the area is habitable and a settlement develops.

- Ismaeel grows up; Prophet Ibraheem (as), in one of his visits to this area, is now commanded by Allah to raise the foundations of the Kabah, which is very close to the well of Zamzam.

- The raising of the Kabah attracts pilgrims, and further develops the area; subsequent developments have now made this area into the international city of Makkah, where at the very least, two million pilgrims come for Hajj annually, at the same spot where Hajar and Ismaeel first came at the command of Allah.

1.2 Qussay

(Refer to Chart 2 on page 251)

- After a gap of some generations - the time zone is now fifth century AD (400-500 AD) - Qussay, from the forefather of Prophet Ibraheem (as), is living in Makkah.

- Let us look at the status of Makkah and the culture of the Arabs in the region of Hejaz (which was predominantly the current Makkah and Madinah areas, and their immediate surrounding areas, in Saudi Arabia).

- Makkah is the centre of the region at the time, visited by two main groups of people from outside of Makkah.

- The first group are the pilgrims, who come for circumambulation of the Kabah; after Prophet Ismaeel (as), the true Islamic practices are slowly forgotten in time and replaced with new practices; people take to idol worshipping and put idols in the Kabah.

- The second group are the traders, as Makkah is the financial centre of the trade in the region, and between the trading routes from the south (Yemen) to the north (Syria).

- There is no particular organised system of administration; things are conducted mainly on a family or tribal basis.

- The lifestyle is nomadic in nature, with family or tribes moving from one area to another periodically, mainly for grazing their animals.

- The people also move around as a result of skirmishes and incursions in areas belonging to different families and tribes.

- There are no systematic arrangements for the provisions of the pilgrims and the traders who come outside of Makkah.

- Qussay is a talented man who has excellent administrative and leadership skills; he uses his talents to initiate a system of administration in Makkah to benefit the local people and the outsiders - the pilgrims and the traders.

- He sets up the following systems, until now not practised in the region:

    1 a hall of chambers - a committee or a council of leaders to make collective decisions;

    2 a code of conduct - a set of rules and regulations (constitution) by which the committee will govern;

    3 a central meeting place - a building in the vicinity of the Kabah where people would gather for meetings, discussions and decision making;

    4 a tax system - this was collected from the local people of Makkah, to raise revenue for the provision of services for the communal benefit, and for the pilgrims and traders coming into Makkah;

    5 a system for providing food, water and shelter to the pilgrims.

- Qussay is so successful in gathering the various local tribes and clans into some sort of a cohesive community that he is given the title of Quresh - the gatherer.

- Qussay is the Chief of the Quresh and also takes on the role as the Custodian of the Kabah, the Head of the Army and the Chairman of the Chambers (committee of tribal/family leaders).

- Quassay leaves his mark in Arabia for his achievements in centralisation, administration and facilitation for the communal good of the locals and the visitors.

1.3 Hashim

(Refer to Chart 2 on page 251)

- After the death of Qussay, his duties now pass to his eldest son, Abd Dar, but he is not an able administrator or an effective leader; so he passes all his inherited duties to his younger brother, Abd Manaf, who has the qualities of leadership and administrative skills.

- When Abd Dar dies, his eldest son Abd Shams wants to take on all the duties that his father had passed on to Abd Manaf; a tribunal is now set up to divide the duties between Abd

Manaf and his nephew, Abd Shams, and the allocation of duties is agreed by all.

- Abd Manaf takes on the duties of providing food and water to the pilgrims and visitors, and he is the Head of the Army. Abd Shams (the son of Abd Dar) takes on the duties of being the Custodian of Kabah, and the flag-bearer of the army in times of war. The Chairman of the Chambers role is shared by the two.

- After the death of Abd Manaf, his duties now pass to his younger son Hashim, rather than to his eldest son Abd Shams who is not an able administrator or an effective leader.

- Hashim is as good as his grand-father Qussay in terms of his leadership and administrative skills.

- Once, a great famine hits Makkah, and Hashim uses his own money to buy bread from outside and provide to the people of Makkah; it is this act of breaking the bread and feeding the people that gives him the title of Hashim (the one who breaks bread); his actual name is Amr.

- Hashim initiates the trade caravans of Quresh from Yemen in the south to Syria and beyond to the north; he personally negotiates its safe passage with various parties along the route at a time when looting and plundering of the caravans is common.

- He manages to ensure safe passage by offering guarantees to these nomadic tribes of the special status and hospitality when they are in Makkah; he also guarantees them reduced prices of the goods delivered to them during the trade journeys.

- Due to his good character and sincere acts for the benefit of the community, Hashim enjoys great popularity and rises to prominence to become the Chief of the Quresh.

- Upon the death of Abd Shams (the elder brother of Hashim), his son Umayya now makes a claim that the duties performed by his uncle Hashim should really all belong to him, as it rightfully should have belonged to his father (Abd Shams) as the eldest son in the family.

- Umayya is envious and jealous of the status enjoyed by Hashim amongst the Quresh; he therefore starts a sustained campaign against Hashim.

- Umayya challenges Hashim to relieve himself of the duties and pass them all to him; it is common knowledge amongst the people of the differences in attitudes and intentions between Umayya and Hashim; Umayya is not suitable for such a position and he wants it for the glory, whereas Hashim uses it to benefit the community.

- A tribunal is now setup to decide who takes over all the duties and the role of Chief of Quresh; a pre-condition is that the loser will be exiled to northern Syria for ten years; the tribunal decides in favour of Hashim, and Umayya is exiled for ten years.

- Therefore, Hashim remains as the Chief of Quresh and continues with his allocated duties.

- When Hashim dies, his role and duties are taken over by one of his sons, Abdul Muttalib, who also rises to great fame amongst the Quresh for his services.

1.4 Ancestors of Imam Husein (as) and Yazeed

(Refer to Chart 2 on page 251)

- Amongst the children of Abdul Muttalib are Abdullah and Abu Talib; one of the sons of Abdullah is Muhammad - Prophet Muhammad (saww). One of the sons of Abu Talib is Ali - Imam Ali (as).

- From the first marriage of Imam Ali (as) to Lady Fatemah (as), the daughter of Prophet Muhammad (saww), they have a son called Husein - Imam Husein (as). It is this Imam Husein (as) that is associated with the tragedy of Karbala.

- One of the sons of Umayya is Harb, and one of the sons of Harb is Abu Sufyan; amongst the children of Abu Sufyan are Yazeed and Muawiya; one of the sons of Muawiya is Yazeed; it is this Yazeed (the son of Muawiya) that is associated with the tragedy of Karbala.

- The whole family originating from Hashim is generally referred to as Banu Hashim, an Arabic term meaning the Children of Hashim; so Imam Husein (as) is a Hashimi.

- The whole family originating from Umayya is generally known as Banu Umayya, an Arabic term meaning the Children of Umayya; so Yazeed is an Umayyad.

1.5 Family tree of Imam Husein (as)

(Refer to Chart 1 on the inside back cover)

- The chart shows the family members of Imam Husein (as); we are looking at his family members who have direct relevance to the tragedy of Karbala; those who do have direct relevance but are not shown on the chart will be discussed at the appropriate point in the text.

- The numbers before the names cross-reference to the text below.

- Note that at the time, it was common for men to have more than one wife at a time, up to a maximum of four, as allowed under Islamic rules.

Family members who died before the tragedy of Karbala:

People shown in back colour and by the symbol ⊠ (refer to Chart 1 on the inside back cover) are not alive when the tragedy of Karbala occurs:

1 Abdul Muttalib
Imam Husein's (as) great grandfather on the father side; he is the grandfather of Imam Ali (as).

2 Abdullah
Imam Husein's (as) great grandfather on the mother side; he is the grandfather of Lady Fatemah (as).

3 Abu Talib
Imam Husein's (as) grandfather on the father side; he is the father of Imam Ali (as) and the uncle of Prophet Muhammad (saww).

4 Prophet Muhammad (saww)
Imam Husein's (as) grandfather on the mother side; he is the father of Lady Fatemah (as).

5 Imam Ali (as)
Imam Husein's (as) father; he is the cousin of Prophet Muhammad (saww).

6 Lady Fatemah (as)
Imam Husein's (as) mother; she is the daughter of Prophet Muhammad (saww).

7 Imam Hasan (as)
Imam Husein's (as) elder brother; he is the eldest son of Imam Ali (as) and Lady Fatemah (as).

8 Jaffer
Imam Husein's (as) uncle; he is Imam Ali's (as) brother and the son of Abu Talib.

9 Aqil
Imam Husein's (as) uncle; he is Imam Ali's (as) brother and the son of Abu Talib.

10 Muhammad
Imam Husein's (as) brother in-law; he is married to Imam Husein's (as) younger sister - Lady Umme Kulthum; he is the son of Jaffer, the uncle of Imam Husein (as).

11 Shahr Banoo
Imam Husein's (as) first wife; mother of Imam Zainul Abideen (as); she is from the royal family of Iran, the daughter of an Iranian King, and came to Madinah when Iran came under the influence of the Muslims; she died soon after the birth of their eldest son, Imam Zainul Abideen (as).

12 Umme Ishaq
Imam Husein's (as) wife; mother of Fatemah Kubra; there is no mention of her being present in Karbala or with the survivors in Kufa and Damascus in the literature; the inference is that she died before the tragedy of Karbala occurs.

13 Laila
Imam Husein's (as) wife; mother of Ali Akbar; there is no mention of her being present in Kufa and Damascus with the survivors in the literature of; there is mention though that Ali

Akbar, her son, was brought up by Lady Zainab; the inference is that Laila died before the tragedy of Karbala occurs; some literature mention of her presence in Karbala, mainly when narrating the martyrdom of her son, Ali Akbar.

14 of Qudaiyah tribe
Imam Husein's (as) wife; her name is not recorded and is untraceable, but she was from the Qudaiyah tribe; again, there is no mention of her being present in Karbala or with the survivors in Kufa and Damascus in the literature; so the inference is she died before the tragedy of Karbala occurs.

15 Jaffer
Imam Husein's (as) son; his mother is the lady of Qudaiyah tribe (mentioned above in person number 14).

16 Laila
Imam Husein's step mother; she is one of the wives of Imam Ali (as), whom she married after the death of his first wife, Lady Fatemah (as); her name is also not mentioned as being present in Karbala or with the survivors in Kufa and Damascus in the literature; so the inference is that she died before the tragedy of Karbala occurs.

17 Saeed

Imam Husein's (as) cousin; he is the son of Aqil, the uncle of Imam Husein (as).

Family members who did not accompany Imam Husein (as)

People shown in pink colour and by the symbol ◎ (refer to Chart 1 on the inside back cover) are alive when the Karbala tragedy occurs; however, they did not accompany Imam Husein (as) when he left Madinah to end up in Karbala:

18 Ummul Baneen

Imam Husein's (as) step mother; she is one of the wives of Imam Ali (as), whom she married after the death of his first wife Lady Fatemah (as); her actual name is Fatemah Kalbiyya; Imam Ali (as) marries her as her tribe is known to produce children known for their bravery, and Imam Ali (as) wishes for a brave son to represent him in his absence at the time of tragedy in Karbala.

19 Abdullah

Imam Husein's (as) brother in-law; he is married to Imam Husein's (as) sister - Lady Zainab; he is the son of Jaffer, the uncle of Imam Husein (as) (note here that the two brothers - Muhammad and Abdullah - marry the two sisters - Lady Umme Kulthum and Lady Zainab); he is too ill for the journey.

20 Fatemah Sughra
Imam Husein's (as) daughter; her mother is Umme Ishaq; she is too ill for the journey.

Family members who survived the tragedy of Karbala

People shown in blue colour and by the symbol ◘ (refer to Chart 1 on the inside back cover) accompany Imam Husein (as) when he leaves Madinah, and they are in Karbala when the tragedy occurs; they survive the tragedy of Karbala and finally return home to Madinah:

21 Zainab
Imam Husein's (as) younger sister; she is the third child of Imam Ali (as) and Lady Fatemah (as); she is fifty five years old when the tragedy of Karbala occurs.

22 Umme Kulthum
Imam Husein's (as) younger sister; she is the fourth child of Imam Ali (as) and Lady Fatemah (as); she is fifty four years old when the tragedy of Karbala occurs.

23 Ali Zainul Abideen (as)
Imam Husein's (as) eldest son; his mother is Shahr Banoo; he is twenty two years old when the tragedy of Karbala occurs.

24 Muhammad Baqir (as)
Imam Husein's (as) grandson; his father is Imam Zainul Abideen (as), the fourth Imam; he

is three years old when the tragedy of Karbala occurs; he is the fifth Imam.

25 Rubab

Imam Husein's (as) wife; she is the mother of three children - Fatemah Sughra, Sukaina, and Ali Asghar.

26 Fatemah Kubra

Imam Husein's (as) eldest daughter; her mother is Umme Ishaq; after the tragedy of Karbala, she gets married to Hasan, the son of Imam Hasan (as).

27 Hasan

Imam Husein's (as) nephew; he is the son of Imam Hasan (as), the second Imam; he is also known as Hasan Muthanna - Hasan the Second, to distinguish him from his father by the same name; he participates in the battle at Karbala, and he is mistakenly taken for dead and survives the tragedy.

Family members who are martyred in Kufa

People shown in green colour and by the symbol ⊗ (refer to Chart 1 on the inside back cover) accompany Imam Husein (as) when he leaves Madinah; they did not get to Karbala but are martyred in Kufa:

28 Muslim

Imam Husein's (as) cousin; he is the son of Aqil; he gets martyred in Kufa, just before the tragedy of Kerbala occurs. A more detailed discussion is given in Chapter 6.

29 Ibraheem

Imam Husein's (as) cousin's son; he is the son of Muslim; Muslim takes two of his youngest sons to Kufa with him; he gets martyred in Kufa with his brother Muhammad, about one year after the tragedy of Karbala; he is no more than twelve years old.

30 Muhammad

Imam Husein's (as) cousin's son; he is the youngest son of Muslim; he is the other son that Muslim takes with him to Kufa; he gets martyred in Kufa with his brother Ibraheem, about one year after the tragedy of Karbala; he is no more than twelve years old.

Family member who dies in Damascus

Person shown in lavender colour and by the symbol ⊕ (refer to Chart 1 on the inside back cover) accompanies Imam Husein (as) when he leaves Madinah, and she is in Karbala when the tragedy occurs; she survives the tragedy of Karbala but dies in Damascus:

31 Sukaina
Imam Husein's (as) daughter; her mother is Rubab; she is about five years old; she is also known by the other names of Sakina or Ruqaiyya.

Family members who are martyred in Karbala

People shown in red colour and by the symbol ● (refer to Chart 1 on the inside back cover) accompany Imam Husein (as) when he leaves Madinah and are with him in Karbala; they are martyred with him in Karbala on the day of Ashura:

32 Qasim
Imam Husein's (as) nephew; he is the son of Imam Hasan (as), the brother of Imam Husein (as); he is about thirteen years old.

33 Ahmed
Imam Husein's (as) nephew; he is the son of Imam Hasan (as), the brother of Imam Husein

(as); he is also known as Abu Bakr; he is about twelve years old.

34 Abdullah
Imam Husein's (as) nephew; he is the son of Imam Hasan (as), the brother of Imam Husein (as); he is about eleven years old.

35 Aun
Imam Husein's (as) nephew; he is about nine years old; he is the son of Abdullah and Lady Zainab, the sister of Imam Husein (as); Aun joins Imam Husein (as) at a place called Tanim (see Section 7.2).

36 Muhammad
Imam Husein's (as) nephew; he is the second son of Abdullah and Lady Zainab, the sister of Imam Husein (as); he is about eight years old and the younger brother to Aun; Muhammad joins Imam Husein (as) at a place called Tanim (see Section 7.2).

37 Abdullah
Imam Husein's (as) cousin's son; he is the son of Muslim, the cousin of Imam Husein (as).

38 Muhammad
Imam Husein's (as) cousin's son; he is the son of Muslim, the cousin of Imam Husein (as).

39 Muhammad

Imam Husein's (as) cousin's son; he is the son of Saeed, the cousin of Imam Husein (as).

40 Abdullah

Imam Husein's (as) cousin; he is the son of Aqil, the uncle of Imam Husein (as).

41 Jaffer

Imam Husein's (as) cousin; he is the son of Aqil, the uncle of Imam Husein (as).

42 Abd Rahman

Imam Husein's (as) cousin; he is the son of Aqil, the uncle of Imam Husein (as).

43 Muhammad

Imam Husein's (as) brother; he is the son of Imam Ali (as) and Laila; he is also known as Muhammad Al-Asghar, the Junior Muhammad, to distinguish from another elder son of Imam Ali (as) also called Muhammad (Muhammad Hanafiyya); he is also known as Abu Bakr.

44 Abbas

Imam Husein's (as) brother; he is the son of Imam Ali (as) and Ummul Baneen.

45 Jaffer

Imam Husein's (as) brother; he is the son of Imam Ali (as) and Ummul Baneen.

46 Othman

Imam Husein's (as) brother; he is the son of Imam Ali (as) and Ummul Baneen.

47 Abdullah

Imam Husein's (as) brother; he is the son of Imam Ali (as) and Ummul Baneen.

48 Ali Akbar

Imam Husein's (as) second son; his mother is Laila.

49 Ali Asghar

Imam Husein's (as) third son; his mother is Rubab; he is also known as Abdullah.

50 Imam Husein (as)

Himself; he is the grand-son of Prophet Muhammad (saww), and the son of Imam Ali (as) and Lady Fatemah (as).

2 Situation During The Prophet's Time

52 BH - 11 AH
570 AD - 632 AD

In this chapter, we will look at the situation in Arabia (principally Makkah and Madinah), during the time when Prophet Muhammad (saww) propagates the message of Islam. A description of the problems he faces during his lifetime is described.

2.1 Before the declaration of Islam

- The area of Hejaz mainly covers the cities of Makkah and Yathrib (as Madinah was known at that time) and their immediate surrounding areas.

- The city of Makkah is the established centre of trade in the region, especially for travelling caravans engaged in business from Yemen in the south to Syria and beyond in the north.

- Over the years, after the time of Prophet Ismaeel (as), people forget the true message of belief in One Allah preached by him; they change to idol worshipping; they put idols in the Kabah; there are as many as 360 idols inside the Kabah, one for each day of the year.

- Makkah is the spiritual centre for the people of Hejaz who come to pray to the idols in the Kabah, and circumambulate the Kabah in reverence to the idols inside.

- Kabah also serves as the centre of literary excellence, where Arabs excelling in poetry come to recite their compositions.

- The whole social system is family and tribal based; loyalty is to the family and tribe, regardless of the merits or justice in any situation; there are many cases reported where for a most trivial misunderstanding or disagreement between families, the situation escalates to a full scale war between the families or tribes.

- The Arabs believe that amongst all the people of the world, they are the superior race, and all the tribes in the region have lesser levels of social standing; the Quresh consider themselves the most superior and elite of all the other tribes, and that their beliefs and customs are sacrosanct.

- As Allah plans it, He sends His Messenger to be born amongst this ruling family in Makkah; Prophet Muhammad (saww) - from now referred to as the Prophet - is born in Makkah in 570 AD, 52 BH.

2.2 Establishing his credentials

- Prophet Muhammad (saww) is born in a community whose beliefs and customs are deep rooted; to change the people to Islamic ways is not going to be possible within a short time.

- So, the Prophet has to live amongst these people in such a manner that they will take him seriously when he does invite them to become Muslims; in other words, he has to win the hearts and minds of the people before making public his mission.

- The Prophet establishes his credentials in three ways - being truthful, being trustworthy, and demonstrating his impeccable character; it takes forty years before Allah instructs him to start his mission.

- The first credential is to establish that he always tells the truth and never ever lies; he does not tell a lie even for the tiniest of anything; in time, people come to know that he can be fully trusted to tell the truth, whatever the situation.

- In a community, where lying is routinely accepted and practised, the Prophet stands out as the one who can be completely relied upon to tell the truth.

- The second credential he establishes is that he is trustworthy in all circumstances.
- It is common practice at the time for people to leave their valuables and money with someone for safekeeping when they go away on a journey; on their return, the person does not always return all the deposits left with him, or does not return any at all; the Prophet always returns in full all that is left in his care.
- In business transactions, it is also common practice for employees to short change their employers; the Prophet always accounts in full all the transactions and never keeps back any goods or money that was not his due.
- So, in a community where treachery and betrayal are commonplace, the Prophet stands out as the one who can be absolutely trusted in all matters.
- The third credential that he establishes is his impeccable character.
- The general behaviour of the people is crude; rudeness amongst them is common; the social behaviour of basic decency in talking and dealing with fellow human beings is not widely practised.
- So in a community where good manners are lacking, the Prophet is a role model of the best

of character, never once resorting to improper manners.

- It is very important that these credentials are firmly established in the peoples' minds so that when the Prophet starts his mission of propagating Islam, the people cannot question his sincerity, integrity and modesty; for the whole message of Islam to be accepted hinges on the people believing in the Prophet.

- Only when the Prophet reaches the age of forty years, does Allah now command him to start his mission of propagating Islam.

2.3 Prophet's message versus current practices

- The Prophet begins his mission, first with his immediate family, and then after three years, with the public in general.

- Until now, the people of Makkah like and respect the Prophet because of his three credentials; they know him as Muhammad, son of Abdullah, and of the Quresh tribe.

- As soon as he starts talking about Islam, a group of people - from now on to be referred to as the opposition (comprising the leaders and rulers of Makkah, people with political influence and connections, people with business interests), start to dislike him, because the message that he is talking about is in conflict with their ways and it is harming their businesses and social standing.

- The message of Islam that the Prophet brings is about the unity of God - there is only One God, Allah, who is unseen and there are no other Gods.

- The Prophet's teaching is that in Islam, all people are equal in the presence of Allah and that they will be judged by their actions and not on their race, or tribal and family connections.

- This message of equality directly contradicts the practices at the time; the community is based on a ruling class, slave-master relationship (as slavery is practised at the time), family prominence, tribal supremacy, and so on.

- The Prophet talks about the Hereafter and the Day of Judgement, and that life in this world should focus on ways to ensure a peaceful Hereafter.

- The practice at the time is to live for this world only, for they do not believe in the Hereafter to come; so, materialistic tendencies and merry making are the focus of life.

- The Islamic teachings of humility and forgiveness in all spheres of community life are propagated by the Prophet.
- The character of the people is opposite to this; people are used to being harsh and rude with each other, and every transgression is not forgotten nor forgiven, but revenge is sought.
- The idea of treating people, including slaves, humanely and with humility is also causing resentment with those who have slaves.
- These are just some examples of Islamic message clashing with the customs and ways practised by the people around the Prophet at the time.

2.4 Opposition in Makkah

- The opposition at first are not alarmed or worried by the message of Islam, however much it clashed with its culture and ways; for in the first three years of propagation, only about forty people have come to the faith.

- However, after the first three years, when the Prophet is now starting to talk publicly about Islam, the opposition sees that many more people are accepting Islam; these people are from across the community and are not confined to any particular tribe, family or social class.

- The opposition see this widespread acceptance of Islam as dangerous, because it threatens their privileges, social standing and business interests; they find it particularly annoying that the man - the Prophet, or Muhammad as they call him - who is threatening their status and lifestyle is himself from the same family and the tribe of Quresh.

- So they embark on a campaign of opposition to stop him from spreading any further the message of Islam; they cannot be too harsh on the Prophet, since his uncle Abu Talib is one of the Quresh chiefs and is extending his patronage and protection to his nephew, the Prophet; they do not want to antagonise Abu

Talib and cause a major rift between the Quresh families.

- The forms of opposition become increasingly sinister with the passing of time, as the Prophet is unstoppable in his propagation and is persuading the people to accept the faith; they embark on six main forms of opposition.

- The first form of opposition involves paying children to throw rubbish and stones at the Prophet when he in the streets; they use the children for two reasons; first, they can claim they have no direct involvement in harming the Prophet; second, they can always say that it is just children playing their childish games in the streets.

- When this action does not stop the Prophet continuing with his propagation, the second stage of opposition is to use psychological tactics by demeaning his character and his actions.

- They call him a magician and a mad man; this is to implant into the minds of the people that they should not take the words of the Prophet seriously; they even place their people on the outskirts of Makkah warning any trader, visitor or pilgrim, not to be fooled by the Prophet's words when they hear him speak near the Kabah.

- The other psychological tact they use is to demean his actions by throwing the carcasses of animals next to him whenever he performs his prayers in public, in front of the Kabah; the intention here is to demean the act of prayer itself.

- When these actions have no effect in slowing down the Prophet, the opposition moves to the third stage of sending hecklers whenever he speaks in public.

- They use two methods; in the first case, they would pay women to start singing near the place where the Prophet is talking about Islam to the people; this causes a distraction and people's attention is then split between listening to the melodious tunes of the women and the voice of the Prophet.

- In the second case, they pay men to join the crowd listening to the Prophet and then heckle him, thereby causing the Prophet's voice not to be heard and disruption to the listening crowd.

- Despite the heckling, more people accept Islam; the opposition realise that for as long as the Prophet is allowed free movement in town, he will not stop inviting people to the faith and they will still come to listen to him.

- So, the fourth stage of opposition moves to a more drastic level – to isolate the Prophet from the public; this order is confirmed in writing, signed by the opposition, and it is hung inside the Kabah.

- The isolation is imposed by sending the Prophet away from the city centre and the Kabah; however, it is not only the Prophet that is to be isolated, but the whole of the Hashimite clan, that is, all the family members of his brothers, uncles and nephews; they move to an area, away from the city centre, belonging to Abu Talib (the uncle of the Prophet).

- The Hashimis are effectively under house arrest and some are only allowed out purchasing food; the isolation lasts for three years; they are released and allowed back to their homes only because of the pressure from some local people, combined with the information from the Prophet that almost all the words on the written order, hung in the Kabah, have been eaten by the ants; after his release from the isolation, the Prophet continues with his propagation of Islam.

- The fifth stage of the opposition is to bribe the Prophet somehow in return for his silence, that is, to stop propagating Islam.

- A delegation from the opposition come to Abu Talib and tell him to offer the Prophet any amount of money, pretty damsels and government office, in return for his silence; the Prophet gives them the famous reply “even if they offer the sun in my right hand, and the moon in my left hand, I will not stop propagating Islam to the last of my breath”.

- When these offers of bribery fail, the opposition even try to entice Abu Talib to hand over to them his nephew, the Prophet, in exchange for a young handsome man from the family of the opposition; Abu Talib naturally turns down this offer.

- Abu Talib dies, and the Prophet now looses the protection and the patronage that shielded him from direct harm by the opposition; however, he is still continuing with his propagation.

- The opposition now move to the sixth stage of planning a murder, as the only way to silence the Prophet.

- A person is chosen from each of the leading tribes of Makkah and is armed with a sword to kill the Prophet when he is in bed at night; a joint murder squad is chosen so no one particular tribe can then be singled out for the murder and targeted for any revenge.

- The Prophet is forewarned of this plan by Allah, and instead Imam Ali (as) takes his place in his bed; when the murderers come in for the kill and lift the bed sheet, they see it is Imam Ali (as) instead of the Prophet and realise their plan has failed.

- On this same night, the Prophet leaves for the city of Yathrib; representatives of some people from Yathrib who accepted Islam, gave him an open invitation to come, live, practise Islam and be their leader in Yathrib; this is the night of Hijrah - Migration, which marks the start of the Islamic calendar (corresponding to 622 AD).

2.5 Opposition in Madinah

- The Prophet, his family and the Muslims who have migrated from Makkah are now settled in Yathrib and most of the people, except of the Jewish faith, accept Islam; Yathrib in turn is renamed Madinah.

- Opposition in Madlnah to Islam is coming from two sources - internal and external; the Prophet successfully deals with the internal opposition led by groups hostile to him, for they fear their loss of economic and political power within Madinah.

- The external hostility is from the same opposition group in Makkah, who see that Islam is now flourishing in Madinah and the surrounding regions.

- The opposition from Makkah is open and aggressive, resulting in three major offensive battles that have to be defended by the Muslims of Madinah.

- The battle of Badr, fought in the plains about eighty miles from Makkah, results in the victory of the Muslims.

- The battle of Ohad, fought in the mountain valley about five miles from Madinah, ends in a stalemate.

- The battle of Khandaq (Trench), fought on the boundary of Madinah, results in the victory of the Muslims; this decisive victory finally demoralises the Makkans who from now on never venture into an open warfare with the Muslims of Madinah.

- In the year 6 AH (628 AD), the Prophet dreams of performing the Umrah (the out-of-season pilgrimage); so together with about fourteen hundred Muslims, they go to Makkah; the authorities there refuse them entry and stop them about ten miles from the city centre, at a place called Hudaybiyya.

- The Prophet is keen, as ever, to reach a peaceful settlement rather than engage in any offensive battle with the authorities; a peace agreement is signed between the Prophet and the Makkan authorities which comes to be known as the Hudaybiyya Treaty; the main points are that the Muslims will return the following year for the Umrah (the out-of-season pilgrimage) and that there will be no hostilities between Madinah and Makkah for ten years.

- When the Makkans break the Hudaybiyya treaty, two years after signing the agreement by financing and arming a nearby community allied to Madinah, the Prophet leads a huge army of Muslims from Madinah to Makkah.

- It is now that the opposition in Makkah realise that they stand no chance against the Muslims, so they accept (some reluctantly, some sincerely, some hypocritically) the Islamic faith; the leaders and the prominent of Makkah become Muslims, the general population also accept the faith.

- The Prophet and Imam Ali (as) clear the Kabah of the idols and it has remained so (from 8 AH, 630 AD) till today; Makkah has since become an exclusively Muslims only city.

2.6 Reconfirming the successor

- In the first three years of Prophethood, the Prophet propagates Islam to selected people and in private; after that, in the fourth year, Allah commands him to propagate openly, first to his family and then to the public at large.

- For propagation within the family, he assembles the family members of Abdul Muttalib clan and invites them to accept his Prophethood and become Muslims.

- He tells them that whoever accepts the Islamic faith and testifies to his Prophethood, will be "my brother, vicegerent and successor".

- Imam Ali (as), who is now thirteen years old, is the only one who stands up three times to publicly reaffirm his acceptance, despite the Prophet telling him each time to sit down, to give others in the gathering a chance to take up the offer.

- So, the Prophet named his successor very early on in Makkah; throughout his lifetime, he is treating Imam Ali (as) with a status and deference deserving of being his successor.

- In the year 10 AH (632 AD), on his way back from the Hajj (the in-season pilgrimage), and by the command of Allah, he stops the people at the cross roads of Ghadeer for an announcement; Ghadeer is a junction where people disperse to go back to their own homeland.

- He tells the people that Allah has commanded him to announce the reconfirmation (in front of the whole public who came with him on this Hajj trip) of Imam Ali (as) as his successor; only after this announcement, is the last verse of the Holy Quran revealed.

2.7 Impressions on Imam Husein (as)

- Imam Husein (as) is born in 4 AH (626 AD) when the Prophet is in Madinah.
- When the Prophet dies in 11 AH (632 AD), Imam Husein (as) is seven years old; some lasting impressions of the Prophet's ways are left on him.
- Let us now examine how they influence the way he deals with the situations leading to Karbala.
- First, he sees that the Prophet does not abandon his mission of propagating Islam, despite all the dangers that he faces; even when his family members are put in harm's

way and made to suffer (when they were under house arrest for three years in Makkah).

- Throughout the tragedy of Karbala, he does exactly the same - he does not abandon his mission; even when he and his family are put in harm's way and are subjected to the most extreme of sufferings.

- Second, he sees that the Prophet deals with people according to their intellect and level of understanding; he interacts differently with Imam Ali (as), with his companions, with the Christians of Najaran, with the opposition and with the nomads.

- Similarly, he talks and deals with the people in the same way; for example, with his family, with his companions, with the soldiers of Hurr, with the soldiers of Yazeed and with the army officers.

- Third, he sees that all the battles fought by the Prophet are defensive and never offensive.

- In Karbala, he ensures that his side does not start the battle; it is the opposite side that starts it.

- Fourth, he sees that as a leader, the Prophet is himself engaged in all the battles and is not simply ordering the troops from the side line.

- On the day of Ashura, he is actively engaged in the battle, right up to the last moment.
- Fifth, he sees that the Prophet pursues to negotiate successfully a peace agreement (Hudaybiyya Treaty) to try and avoid bloodshed, but without compromising his mission.
- In Karbala, he also tries his best to avoid any bloodshed without compromising his mission.
- Sixth, he sees that once an agreement is signed, the Prophet honoured it to the letter.
- At one point, he does not agree with the wishes of the people of Kufa for him to go there and become their leader, as this would have broken the earlier agreement between Imam Hasan (as) and Muawiya.

3 Situation During Imam Ali's (as) Time

11 AH - 40 AH
632 AD - 661 AD

In this chapter, we will look at the situation in Arabia, from the time the Prophet dies to the time of Imam Ali's (as) death. In the times in-between, four people become the leader of the Muslims; we will trace the main issues of the time under each leader.

3.1 Immediately after the Prophet's death

- Upon the death of the Prophet, the Muslims are divided into two groups.

- One group is in shock and mourning; these are the overwhelming Muslim population of Madinah, including the family of the Prophet; some members of the Prophet's family are attending to the preparations for the washing, shrouding and burial of the Prophet's body; the rest of the people from within this group are just dazed with sadness, waiting for the burial of the Prophet.

- The other group of people meet in a hall, belonging to the tribe of Saada - Saqifa Banu Saada - away from the city centre, to discuss who should succeed the Prophet as a leader of the Muslims; this hall and event is infamously known as the Saqifa.

- As discussed in the previous chapter, the Prophet has clearly reaffirmed at Ghadeer his earlier announcements that his successor will be Imam Ali (as); however, this group of people from Madinah assemble at Saqifa, away from the city centre and from the Prophet's Mosque, where all discussions affecting the Muslim State are normally held.

- The majority of the people meeting in Saqifa are there for the sole purpose to ignore the command of the Prophet for Imam Ali (as) to be his successor, and to appoint their own man to succeed him; within this gathering, there are four sub-groups, each with their own choice of who the successor should be.

- The whole group in Saqifa is predominantly made up of the indigenous local people of Madinah (who are called the Ansars - the Helpers, for extending their help to the Muslims to migrate from Makkah to Madinah), numbering about three hundred and fifty; there are only three people who are the immigrants (they are called the Muhajirs - the people who came from Makkah to settle in Madinah).

- The locals who are in Saqifa are there because they came to know that some immigrants from Makkah have pre-planned to make one of their own prominent man to succeed the Prophet and deny Imam Ali (as) the leadership reaffirmed at Ghadeer; they are not ready to see a man from Makkah (other than one from their own tribe, or for a few, Imam Ali (as)) to rule over them in their own country.

- The Muslim Arab population in Madinah is divided mainly into two major tribes - the Aws and the Khazraj; there is a third group who retain their Jewish faith and do not accept Islam.

- The first sub-group in Saqifa are the people from the local tribe of Aws; they have come with their leader and lobby for him to be the successor to the Prophet.

- The second sub-group in Saqifa are the people from the local tribe of Khazraj; they have come with their leader and lobby for him to be the successor to the Prophet.

- The third sub-group in Saqifa are people from both tribes (of Aws and Khazraj), and they have come to lobby for Imam Ali (as) to be the successor to the Prophet.

- When the news of the gathering in Saqifa reaches the Prophet's mosque, three people, all originally from Makkah and prominent companions of the Prophet, leave the mosque and head towards Saqifa; they are Abu Bakr, Umar and Abu Ubaydah al-Jarrah; this forms the fourth (and the smallest) sub-group of people in Saqifa.

- In Saqifa, amongst the four sub-groups, there is a lot of shouting and arguing; jealousies and rivalries between the tribes of Madinah also surface at the meeting; each sub-group is arguing for its own man to be chosen as the successor to the Prophet.

- The main reasons given by the fourth sub-group (the three people from Makkah), in and after Saqifa, are that the successor must be from the tribe of Quresh, an early convert to Islam, a near relation to the Prophet, and who shared the early hardships endured by the Prophet.

- The sub-group of people who have come to lobby for Imam Ali (as) say that these four criteria are indeed met by Imam Ali (as), and so he should be the successor to the Prophet; this is set aside and ignored.

- The meeting ends with Abu Bakr emerging as the successor to the Prophet.

- When the business at Saqifa finishes, the Prophet is already buried.

- Imam Ali (as) is now asking the new leader why he has been sidelined at Saqifa; he reminds them that the Prophet had proclaimed in public that his successor is Imam Ali (as); he also tells them that the criteria set by them at Saqifa are more applicable to him rather than to Abu Bakr.

- He is told that he is too young for the office; Imam Ali (as) reminds them the Prophet had chosen leaders based on their ability and not on their age; for example, after the conquest of Makkah, he appointed a young man of twenty years to be in charge; just before his death, he appointed a young man of eighteen years to lead a military campaign.

- Imam Ali (as) is also told later on, that the Quresh would not agree to have the office of Prophethood and Leadership go to the same family, despite of their merit.

3.2 Meaning of Khalifa

- The successor to the Prophet is given the title of Khalifa; the office of the Khalifa is known as the Khilafat.

- Khilafat, in its true sense, comprises three parts.

- The first part is *Imamate*; this is Spiritual Leadership, where the person is able to lead and guide the public in all matters related to religious ways and rules; he needs to be completely knowledgeable and never prone to making even the smallest of mistake of misrepresentation of any aspect of religion; this quality is God-given and cannot be assumed by man himself.

- The second part is *Wilayat*; this is Spiritual Authority, where the person demands absolute obedience from the public in all matters relating to religious ways and rules; his word and commands are then binding to the people who should follow him without questioning his authority; again, he needs to be completely knowledgeable and never prone to making even the smallest of mistake or misrepresentation on any aspect of religion; this quality is also God-given, and cannot be assumed by man himself.

- The third part is *Mulukiyat*; this is Political and Social Leader of a nation (in current times, it is the Prime Minister or President), where the person is the political leader of a community and is in charge of all its political and social administration; this responsibility need not be God-given, but can be allocated by fellow men.

- So, in every sense of the word, Prophet Muhammad (saww) is a Khalifa in addition to being a Prophet, and Imam Ali (as) is a Khalifa, as proclaimed by the Prophet at the command of Allah.

- The office assumed by Abu Bakr and all subsequent leaders who are not from the Prophet's Household (Ahlul Bayt) is the *Mulukiyat* part of the Khilafat, that is, the political and social leadership of the community or nation; however, the title of Khalifa has been given to these political and social leaders of the Muslims.

- Therefore, in order not to confuse the true meaning of the title Khalifa from the title given to those who were responsible only for the political and social leadership role, we will from now on refer to them as Leaders, since their office was not that of a Khalifa (which includes all the three parts of Spiritual

Leadership, Spiritual Authority and Political/Social Leadership).

3.3 Response of Imam Ali (as)

- Imam Ali (as) is turned down for the office of Khilafat, even after he explains his merits and his right to it since the Prophet has publicly proclaimed him to be his successor.

- Imam Ali (as) now has to make a choice - to support or oppose the leadership of Abu Bakr.

- Imam Ali's (as) immediate family members (the Hashimis) and his friends, including some who are the companions of the Prophet, are ready to join Imam Ali (as) should he wish to actively oppose Leader Abu Bakr and his officials.

- Abu Sufyan (see Chart 3 on page 253), a prominent elder from the Umayya family, comes to Imam Ali (as) and promises him the support of the Umayya members should Imam Ali (as) wish to oppose the new leadership; Imam Ali (as) rejects this offer, knowing the mischief making intention of Abu Sufyan.

- Imam Ali (as) makes a choice; one that would be of benefit to Islam, and not for his own personal gain or fame.

- He decides not to oppose Leader Abu Bakr for the office, for doing this would tremendously harm the Islamic movement, still in its infancy, and especially so soon after the Prophet's death.

- However, Imam Ali (as) is very clear in his mind that by not opposing Leader Abu Bakr, he has not given away his own Spiritual Leadership and Spiritual Authority of the Khilafat; the only part of the Khilafat that he is conceding is the Political Leadership.

- He does not stop guiding people, who come to him, on any religious issue; he even offers his advice and guidance to Leader Abu Bakr and subsequent Leaders, who turn to him.

3.4 During Leader Abu Bakr's time

- The time period is 11-13 AH (632-634 AD).

- During the time of the Prophet, many communities around Madinah and Makkah are allied to the government of Madinah in some form.

- Some communities accepted the Islamic faith; they pay tax to the central government in Madinah for protection against any aggression; they also pay an additional tax which is then redistributed to all communities depending on their needs.

- Some communities have not accepted the Islamic faith; they pay a higher tax to the central government in Madinah for protection against any aggression.

- After the death of the Prophet and when Leader Abu Bakr takes over, many such communities refuse to pay any tax to the central government in Madinah; they give two reasons.

- First, they only paid the tax due to the status of the Prophet and are now not willing to continue paying after his death; some communities that had accepted Islam say they will continue to practise Islam, but will not contribute to the central tax in Madinah; a relatively fewer communities say they will no longer practise Islam and will thus not contribute to any central tax.

- Second, some communities say they will only continue with the previous arrangements if the Leader is Imam Ali (as), as proclaimed by the Prophet, and will not recognise the authority of any other leader.

- Leader Abu Bakr, against the advice of his own officials, embarks on a military campaign to bring these communities under the control of the central government in Madinah.

- So starts the first civil war between Muslims of Madinah and its surrounding communities; the government is saying these communities are apostates (an apostate is one who rejects the faith after having accepted it; it is a grave crime in Islam to be an apostate); in reality, only a very small number of communities reject the faith; in Islamic history books, these wars are wrongly referred to as the apostasy wars.

- The civil wars are to the advantage of the government of Madinah.

- First, the internal unease about the way Leader Abu Bakr has come to the office is neutralised by the desire of the public to unite and fight the external campaign.

- Second, the aggressive campaigns are more agreeable to the earlier lifestyle of the Arab population, rather than the peaceful coexistence fostered by the Prophet.

- Third, each victorious campaign brings the spoils of war which are shared by the participating soldiers of Madinah, thereby ensuring the support of the army to the government of the day.

- Fourth, the central government is assured of the income from the taxes paid by these surrounding communities who are now under the control of the government of Madinah.

- When the surrounding communities are brought under the control of the Madinah government, the army is gaining confidence in its military strength and is looking for campaigns further afield in order to gain the spoils of war; Leader Abu Bakr approves of these campaigns and starts what comes to be known as the expansion of the Muslim Empire.

- The Madinah army would give three choices to the population coming under its campaign; first, accept the faith of Islam and pay a central tax to Madinah and enjoy its protection; second, retain their own religious practices but pay a higher central tax to Madinah and enjoy its protection; third, engage in a battle until one side wins.

- The Madinah army units, under various military officers are sent to two fronts; the first front is the Lower Mesopotamia, the present-day southern Iran/Iraq border; this area comes under the control of Madinah during the lifetime of Leader Abu Bakr; the second front is Greater Syria, the present-day Syria, Palestine and Jordan; Leader Abu Bakr dies just as the Madinah army is poised for a victory in Syria.

- Leader Abu Bakr sent an army unit to Syria led by Yazeed, the son of Abu Sufyan who, until the conquest of Makkah, was opposing Islam and the Prophet); Yazeed is the elder brother of Muawiya (see Chart 2 on page 251).

- Just before his death, Leader Abu Bakr appoints Umar (son of Khattab) who was with him at Saqifa, as the next leader; this time, there is no apparent election, selection or consultation; it is a personal appointment by one fallible man to another.

- Imam Ali (as) objects to this personal appointment and for the second time, he explains his merits for the office and the fact that the Prophet publicly proclaimed him to be his successor; for the second time, he is not granted the office.

- The rule of Leader Abu Bakr lasts for two years, from 11 to 13 AH (632 to 634 AD), when he dies.

3.5 During Leader Umar's time

- The time period is 13-23 AH (634-644 AD).
- Leader Umar continues the military campaigns started by Leader Abu Bakr.
- The Syrian campaign, which was on the verge of victory when Leader Abu Bakr dies, ends victoriously under Leader Umar.
- Leader Umar sends the Madinah army to venture deep into the Upper Mesopotamia (present-day Iraq), and the Persian Empire (present-day Iran); on the western front, the Madinah army goes to present-day Egypt.
- By the end of Leader Umar's rule, the Muslim Empire extends to present-day Iran, Iraq, Palestine, Jordan, Syria and Egypt.
- Yazeed, the son of Abu Sufyan, who led the Madinah army to Syria dies in 18 AH; Leader Umar appoints Yazeed's younger brother, Muawiya, the second son of Abu Sufyan (see Chart 2 on page 251) to be the governor of Syria.
- Leader Umar is attacked and wounded by a person who is essentially aggrieved by the taxes that he has to pay; Leader Umar survives for a few days before he dies; during this time,

he sets up a new system to choose his successor.

- He forms a committee of six members; they are to deliberate amongst themselves within a set terms of reference and come up with the next leader; Imam Ali (as) is one of the six members.

- A detailed historical analysis of the composition of this committee shows clearly the bias against Imam Ali (as) and how the conditions imposed on the committee were to ensure that Imam Ali (as) does not win the leadership.

- Four candidates drop out for one reason or another, and the choice is between Imam Ali (as) and Othman (the son of Affan); the final selection criteria are that the leadership will go to the one who agrees to follow the rules of the Quran, the ways of the Prophet and the previous two leaders.

- Imam Ali (as) and Othman both agree to follow the rules of the Quran and the ways of the Prophet; Imam Ali (as) refuses to follow the ways of the previous two leaders, but Othman agrees to it; so the leadership goes to Othman.

- Imam Ali (as) objects to this appointment, and for the third time, he explains his merits for the office and the fact that the Prophet publicly proclaimed him to be his successor; for the third time, he is not granted the office.

- It appears that the old rivalry between the Hashimis and the Umayyas is being kept alive by the governing authorities; first, by denying Imam Ali (as) (a Hashimi) the political and social leadership; second, by giving the governorship of Syria twice (first to Yazeed and then to his younger brother Muawiya) to an Umayya member; thirdly, by having Othman as the third leader who is also from the family of Umayya. (see Chart 3 on page 253).

- The rule of Leader Umar lasts for ten years, from 13 to 23 AH (634 to 644 AD), when he dies.

3.6 During Leader Othman's time

- The time period is 23-35 AH (644-656 AD).

- Leader Othman expands the Muslim Empire on the eastern front by venturing into present-day Afghanistan, and on the western front into northern Africa - Libya, Sudan and Morocco, and into present Cyprus.

- He proves to be of a different character from the previous two leaders in that he uses his position to favour his family members and friends by giving them government positions and public money.

- This open favouritism and misuse of the public treasury cause a lot of resentment amongst the public in various provinces.

- He also gives a free hand to his cousin, Muawiya in Syria, to govern as he wishes with no restraint and control from the central Madinah government; such a free reign is not given to the other governors in the Muslim Empire.

- Muawiya is thus able to consolidate his own personal power and influence in Syria; in time, Syria becomes a self-governing province with no connection to the central Madinah government.

- Over the twelve years Leader Othman is in power, he refuses to take the advice of many well-wishers, including Imam Ali (as), that he should change his ways.

- The public resentment, mainly from the people of Madinah, Kufa, Basra and Egypt, grows and results in a revolt against him; groups of people, mainly from Kufa, Basra and Egypt, come to Madinah to protest against him; the Egyptian group takes the lead in rising against him.

- A delegation of protesters from the Egyptian group surrounds his house and lays a siege by not allowing any food and water supplies to reach him.

- Imam Ali (as) instructs his sons Hassan and Husein to take water to him; they are allowed to pass through because of their status as the Prophet's grand-children and of their father Imam Ali (as); also the protestors do not want to antagonise any member of the Hashimi family.

- Some of the people surrounding the house of Leader Othman finally get inside and kill him.

- The rule of Leader Othman lasts for twelve years, from 23 to 35 AH (644 to 656 AD), when he dies.

3.7 During Imam Ali's (as) time

- The time period is 35-40 AH (656-661 AD).
- There is now an overwhelming majority of people asking Imam Ali (as) to be the next leader; he had asked for this office on three different occasions previously as rightfully belonging to him, but was denied each time.
- This time round, he says he does not want the office of Political Leadership; he sees that the provinces are not being governed properly, mainly due to the governors not being suitable for these positions.
- However, the people do not take no for an answer; Imam Ali (as) therefore agrees on the condition that he will change the governors and rule strictly according to Islamic principles – the rules of the Quran and the ways of the Prophet.
- Imam Ali (as) therefore becomes the fourth leader after the Prophet; he now takes over as a true successor (Khalifa) of the Prophet for he combines the Spiritual Leadership, Spiritual Authority and Political Leadership in one person and office.
- As a Khalifa, Imam Ali (as) brings calm to the city of Madinah after the murder of Leader

Othman; he starts replacing the governors of the provinces and chooses people who are suitable for the posts based on their merits and who will govern according to Islamic ways.

- He removes the governors in the main provinces; Muawiya, the governor of Syria, is one of the governors who refuses to step down.

- In the five years of rule by Imam Ali (as), he faces opposition from three fronts, resulting in three civil wars between Muslims.

- The first opposition comes from Makkah; this is led by Lady Ayesha (one of the wives of the Prophet, and daughter of Leader Abu Bakr) who is in Makkah at the time; she had wished for Talha to be the fourth leader after Leader Othman's death.

- She is supported by two prominent people, Talha and Zubayr; both were part of the six candidates committee in choosing the third leader; both are aspiring for provincial governorship under Imam Ali (as), but he does not give it to them.

- They use the excuse that Leader Othman was innocently murdered, that Imam Ali (as) is not bringing his murderers to justice and in order to seek justice, he must be fought and removed from the office.

- The actual murderers of Leader Othman have since run away and their whereabouts are unknown (other reports say that some of them were killed after killing Leader Othman, while the others escaped); Imam Ali (as) also says that he cannot punish the rest of the hundreds of protestors as they had no actual part in the murder itself, and they have since gone back to Egypt, Kufa and Basra.

- Lady Ayesha, Talha, Zubayr and their supporters go to Basra to mobilise an army to fight Imam Ali (as); Imam Ali (as) mobilises his army from Madinah and goes to Basra to meet Lady Ayesha's army.

- In 36 AH (656 AD) a battle takes place just outside Basra; this is known as the Battle of the Camel (Battle of Jamal), as most fighting occurs around the camel seated by Lady Ayesha; thus the first civil war (between Muslims) during Imam Ali's (as) rule takes place; it is the second civil war between Muslims as the first one occurred during the time of Leader Abu Bakr.

- The Battle of the Camel is won by Imam Ali (as); Talha and Zubayr are killed, and Imam Ali (as) instructs that Lady Ayesha is escorted back to Madinah respectfully.

- Mainly for military strategic reasons, Imam Ali (as) now moves the government headquarters from Madinah (in Arabia) to Kufa (in Iraq).

- The second opposition Imam Ali (as) faces comes from Muawiya, the governor of Syria; he is in this position now for twenty two years, since 18 AH (639 AD), and has enjoyed complete autonomy from the central government in Madinah.

- Muawiya wanted to be the leader of the Muslims after Leader Othman, but now sees that it is Imam Ali (as) who has become the leader; he therefore refuses to recognise Imam Ali (as) as the leader and to step down as the governor as Imam Ali (as) wishes.

- He therefore starts a campaign, within Syria, to discredit Imam Ali (as) by using the same tactics as Lady Ayesha - since Imam Ali (as) is not bringing the murderers of Leader Othman to justice, then he must be fought and removed from the office.

- He also displays the blood soaked shirt which Leader Othman was wearing when he was killed, as a constant reminder to the Syrians of his murder and uses this to stir up animosity towards Imam Ali (as).

- He leads an army from Syria to confront Imam Ali (as) who leads an army from Kufa to confront him; they meet at a place called Siffin, just outside the Syrian border; this is known as the Battle of Siffin, in the year 37 AH (657 AD).

- The second civil war during Imam Ali's (as) rule takes place (and the third in the Islamic history) and ends with a stalemate; that is, no side wins decisively.
- A conciliation agreement (arbitration) is reached between the two parties and further war is stopped.
- The third opposition Imam Ali (as) faces comes from within his own supporters who are not happy with the arbitration achieved; this group comes to be known as the Khawarij (the Seceders), the breakaway group.
- They engage in a battle with Imam Ali's (as) army outside Kufa at a place called Nahrawan; this is known as the Battle of Nahrawan, fought in the year 38 AH (658 AD).
- The third civil war during Imam Ali's (as) rule takes place (and the fourth in the Islamic history) and it ends with a victory for the side of Imam Ali (as).
- Muawiya continues to destabilise the government of Imam Ali (as) by armed

incursions to provinces in Iraq and to Yemen; the Khawarij also continue to cause unrest.

- Two years after the confrontation with the Khawarij at Nahrawan, Imam Ali (as) is killed by one of the Khawarij in 40 AH (661 AD); (the plan was to kill Imam Ali (as), Muawiya and Amr-Aas (the governor of Egypt) at the same time, but Muawiya and Amr-Aas survive the attempt).

- The rule of Imam Ali (as) lasts for five years, from 35 to 40 AH (656 to 661 AD), when he dies.

3.8 Impressions on Imam Husein (as)

- When Imam Ali (as) dies in 40 AH (661 AD), Imam Husein (as) is thirty six years old; some lasting impressions are left on him of Imam Ali's (as) ways.

- Let us now examine how they influence the way he deals with the situations leading to Karbala.

- First, Imam Husein (as) sees that Imam Ali (as) does not abandon his responsibilities of Spiritual Leadership and Spiritual Authority even when he is denied the office of the Political Leadership.

- He does exactly the same thing during his time; when the Political Office is denied to him (by Muawiya and Yazeed), he still carries on with the responsibilities of Spiritual Leadership and Spiritual Authority.

- Second, he sees that Imam Ali (as) does not submit to any conditions which are contrary to Islamic ways in order to obtain the office of the Political Leadership (when Imam Ali (as) refuses to agree to rule according to the ways of the previous two leaders when the third leader was chosen).

- When Yazeed asks Imam Husein (as) for allegiance to his rule, he refuses to do so as the ways of Yazeed are un-Islamic.

- Third, he sees from Imam Ali (as) that a Muslim leader must lead according to the rules of the Quran and the ways of the Prophet.

- He follows this example throughout the time of about ten years when he is the Spiritual Leader and Spiritual Authority of the people.

- Fourth, he sees that Imam Ali (as) does not compromise on any Islamic principle in order to gain popularity in his dealings with the people.

- He uses this principle in refusing to give allegiance to Yazeed, knowing full well that this will be unpopular with some people and lead to his martyrdom.

- Fifth, he sees that all the three battles fought by Imam Ali (as) are defensive and never offensive.

- In Karbala, he ensures that his side does not start the battle; it is the opposite side that start it.

4 Situation During Imam Hasan's (as) Time

40 AH - 50 AH
661 AD - 670 AD

In this chapter, we will look at the situation during the ten year period, between the deaths of Imam Ali (as) and Imam Hasan (as). We will detail the methods used by Muawiya to sideline Imam Hasan (as) to become the leader of the Muslims. The reasons for Imam Hasan's (as) policy during this time will also be discussed.

4.1 Tactics of Muawiya

- The time period is 40-50 AH (661-670 AD).
- Imam Hasan's (as) government (and the whole family of Imam Ali (as)) is based in Kufa (in Iraq) since the time Imam Ali (as) moved there.
- Upon the death of Imam Ali (as), the office of Khalifa (that is Spiritual Leadership, Spiritual Authority and Political leadership), by command of Allah, goes to his elder son, Imam Hasan (as) (see Chart 1 on the inside back cover).

- The people in Arabia and Iraq accept him as their leader without any opposition.

- Muawiya, the powerful governor of Syria, who is aspiring to be the leader since the time of Leader Othman sees that the people in Arabia and Iraq have again not chosen him; he refuses to recognise Imam Hasan (as) as the leader of the Muslims.

- Muawiya, a very clever politician, plans to destabilise and weaken the government of Imam Hasan (as) and then taking over the leadership; he uses four tactics to achieve this.

- First, he uses the media of the time (Friday sermons) in Syria to spread propaganda about the character of Imam Hasan (as); he then ensures that the propaganda filters through from Syria to Arabia and Iraq using his network of spies and paid informants in these countries.

- He attacks Imam Hasan's (as) character by saying he is a womaniser, his government is corrupt and anti-Islamic in its ways.

- Second, Muawiya infiltrates Imam Hasan's (as) government in Kufa by two means; first, he sends Syrians as spies to find jobs in the government departments in Kufa and plants his spies among the local population (in fact, he already had a network of spies in the main cities of Arabia and Iraq since the time of Imam Ali's (as) government, so he now increases their number); second, he builds up a network of paid informants of people already working in the government departments who then send information back to Syria.

- Third, he infiltrates Imam Hasan's (as) army in the lower ranks by the same two tactics; sending Syrians to become private soldiers in the army and recruiting soldiers from within Imam Hasan's (as) army as paid informants with their loyalty to him rather than Imam Hasan (as).

- Fourth, he recruits high ranking officers in Imam Hasan's (as) army with a promise of large amounts of money to defect to him when called upon.

4.2 Muawiya prepares his army

- Imam Hasan (as) is aware of the spy network and the infiltration into his army; he writes to Muawiya to stop this interference.

- Muawiya replies by saying that the office of Khalifa of the Muslims belongs to him and not Imam Hasan (as) as he (Imam Hasan (as)) is not suitable for this office.

- Muawiya writes to Imam Hasan (as) outlining his family genealogy and that he (Muawiya) is more suited to the office and that if Imam Hasan (as) does not step down, then Muawiya will assemble his Syrian army and do battle with Imam Hasan (as); the Syrian army is the best equipped and trained in the region at the time.

- Muawiya then writes to Imam Hasan (as) to come to some kind of agreement to avoid a war between the two armies (we see here that the idea of some kind of a peace agreement is initially suggested by Muawiya).

- Imam Hasan (as) replies by emphasising his family genealogy and its services to Islam, and that he (Imam Hasan (as)) is better qualified than Muawiya to retain the office.

- There follows a series of correspondence between the two parties over a period of about five months in 40-41 AH (661 AD).

- Muawiya mobilises his army of about sixty thousand soldiers to send to the open plains of Maskan (in present-day Iraq) which is a suitable base for such a huge army.

- As the direct route between Syria and Kufa is of unsuitable terrain for such a huge army, the army heads via Mousil in Iraq (not the same as the city of Mosul in present-day northern Iraq) and then southwards towards Maskan.

- Muawiya instructs his commanders to proceed to Maskan slowly for three reasons.

- First, he wants to draw out Imam Hasan's (as) army from Kufa and assess the strength of his army.

- Second, he wants to parade his superior and well equipped army as a show of strength and intimidate Imam Hasan (as) into submission.

- Third, he wants to make his intention to go to war known if Imam Hasan (as) chooses not to step down from the office.

4.3 Imam Hasan (as) prepares his army

- On hearing of Muawiya's army movements, Imam Hasan (as) mobilises his army in Kufa.

- The army of Imam Hasan (as) is made up of mainly three groups of soldiers.

- The first group are the true followers of Imam Hasan (as), for they truly believe in his Spiritual Leadership and Spiritual Authority, and are ready to fight for Imam Hasan (as) to the end.

- The second group are the Khawarij (the Seceders - the breakaway group); they missed their earlier chance to murder Muawiya and Amr-Aas (the governor of Egypt) when the plan was to kill them and Imam Ali (as) at the same time; so they now see an opportunity to kill Muawiya by joining the army of Imam Hasan (as).

- The third group are the mercenaries - the soldiers of fortune - who have joined the army simply to benefit from the spoils of war.

- Imam Hasan (as) sends an advance army of about twelve thousand soldiers to Maskan, under the command of Ubaydullah (son of Abbas Abdul Muttalib, see Chart 4 on page 255) and his deputy commander is Qays Saad; the instructions to Ubaydullah are not to start the battle, but act defensively if Muawiya starts it.

- As Imam Hasan (as) is aware that some of his army officers have switched their loyalty to Muawiya, he chooses Ubaydullah for his loyalty to Imam Hasan (as) for two reasons.

- First, they are related, as Ubaydullah's father is the uncle of the Prophet, the grand-father of Imam Hasan (as) (see Chart 4 on page 255); he is therefore not likely to turn against Imam Hasan (as).

- Second, Ubaydullah's two sons were earlier killed in Yemen by Muawiya's forces; so Ubaydullah has a very good reason not to side with Muawiya.

- Meanwhile, Imam Hasan (as) camps at Nukhayla, just outside Kufa, and mobilises more troops as the support army.

- Imam Hasan (as) then heads to Madayn, a city about twenty miles south east of Baghdad and about forty five miles from Maskan, and makes Madayn as his base; he has about eight thousand soldiers with him.

- Madayn is strategically positioned as a supply route to Kufa from Iran and this therefore acts as a last post of defence.

4.4 What happens at Maskan

- At Maskan, the two armies are now facing each other; Muawiya has about sixty thousand soldiers and Ubaydullah for Imam Hasan (as) has about twelve thousand soldiers.

- Muawiya gives instructions not to start the battle, even though he could probably easily win the battle as he has about five times more soldiers with him; he does this mainly for two reasons.

- First, he does not want to be seen to obtain the leadership of the Muslims by force, by winning a battle against Imam Hasan (as); he wants to get it by peaceful means so as to legitimise his claim to the office.

- Second, by avoiding a battle, he wants to win the "hearts and minds" of the people so as to be seen as the saviour of the Muslims, thereby further legitimising his claim to office.

- He embarks on two fronts to achieve this; first, he starts bribing Imam Hasan's (as) army to change sides; second, he spreads misinformation (that Imam Hasan (as) has already agreed to a peace agreement) to demoralise Imam Hasan's (as) army.

- He sends word to Ubaydullah (commander of Imam Hasan's (as) army in Maskan) that he should change sides and come over to him and that he will pay him one million dirhams (some reports say one hundred thousand dirhams); half is to be paid as soon as he changes side and the other half when Muawiya enters Kufa; this is a lot of money even by today's standards.

- Ubaydullah agrees to betray Imam Hasan (as) and he changes side at night; Imam Hasan's (as) army realise this in the morning and the deputy commander, Qays Saad takes charge.

- Muawiya persuades Imam Hasan's (as) soldiers in Maskan that they should also change sides as their commander did; he says there is no point in fighting him as Imam Hasan (as) has agreed to a peace arrangement anyway (which was not true) and that he would pay them money.

- About eight thousand (of the twelve thousand) soldiers change sides to Muawiya; this completely destroys the effectiveness of Imam Hasan's (as) army in Maskan.

- Qays Saad sends word of the developments in Maskan to Imam Hasan (as) in Madayn.

4.5 What happens at Madayn

- Imam Hasan (as) gets the report from Qays Saad of the defection of his commander and about two thirds of his army to Muawiya.

- The army in Madyan also come to hear about this and they in turn are getting restless.

- Muawiya sends three of his men to Imam Hasan (as) in Madyan: Mughira Shuba, Abdullah Amir Kurayz and Abd-ar-Rahman al-Hakam.

- They come to Sabat (an area in Madyan) and meet with Imam Hasan (as) in his camped tent.

- Muawiya's message to Imam Hasan (as) is to stop planning for a battle as his commander and most of his army in Maskan have changed sides; he also sends letters from the officers in Maskan informing him that there are officers in the Madayn army who are ready to kill Imam Hasan (as) at the word of Muawiya; the only option open to Imam Hasan (as) is to make a peace agreement with Muawiya and hand over the office to him.

- A blank paper, signed by Muawiya at the bottom, is given to Imam Hasan (as) for him to write down the terms of the peace agreement as he would like them.

- When the three men come out of the tent, they deliberately discuss their conversations they had with Imam Hasan (as) in a loud voice so that the soldiers gathered around the tent hear of it.

- When the soldiers hear of this, they start to mutiny and talk about leaving Imam Hasan (as) and joining Muawiya or returning to Kufa; this is precisely what Muawiya had planned for.

- The Khawarij (Seceders - the breakaway group) see this as selling out to Muawiya by Imam Hasan (as) (in the same way, as they saw it from their point of view, the selling out to Muawiya by Imam Ali (as) in Siffin).

- Some of these soldiers go into the tent of Imam Hasan (as) and they rob his belongings, his outer garments and even his prayer mat.

- They accuse him of being a "kafir" - an unbeliever. One of them, Jarrah Sinan, attacks Imam Hasan (as) with an axe, cutting deep into the bone of his thigh; he has to be put on a stretcher and moved from the Sabat site to the White Palace (as the grand mansion of the governor of Madayn's residence was called - initially belonging to the Persian royalty).

- He accuses him and his father (Imam Ali (as)) to be a "mushrik" - a polytheist.

4.6 The reasons for a peace agreement

- Imam Hasan (as) now considers his options; whether to go to battle against Muawiya with his remaining army in Madayn and Maskan who are demoralised and in disarray, and being certain of even more defections and betrayal from them; or, to take up the offer from Muawiya for some sort of peace agreement with him.

- He decides that coming to a peace agreement with Muawiya is the best option for the well being and long term survival of Islam.

- The two parties want a peace agreement for different reasons.

- Imam Hasan (as) wants it for two reasons.

- First, to avoid the complete destruction of his remaining army by Muawiya's forces (and the traitors who have now defected).

- Second, he wants to draft the terms of the peace agreement in such a way that they will expose the hypocrisy and the duplicity of Muawiya who is portraying himself as the good Muslim and the saviour of Islam.

- Muawiya wants the peace agreement to be in place for two reasons also.

- Firstly, by not engaging in a battle, he wants to be seen as the person who avoided the spilling of Muslim blood, thereby increasing his stature and leadership credibility in the Muslim world.

- Second, he sees the peace agreement as a way to legitimise his bid for the leadership of the Muslims.

- He is so intent on getting some form of peace agreement in order to achieve his two objectives above, that he even presented Imam Hasan (as) with a signed blank paper and allowed Imam Hasan (as) to unilaterally set down the terms of the agreement.

4.7 The peace agreement

- The peace agreement between Imam Hasan (as) and Muawiya is sometimes referred to as the peace treaty.

- There are six main points to the agreement; we will look at each point and see if the terms of agreement are kept or broken.

Point 1: Muawiya is to rule according to the rules of Quran and the ways of the Prophet.

- The fact that this has to be mentioned at all means that Muawiya is at present not doing so (that is governing Syria according to the rules of the Quran and the ways of the Prophet).
- Imam Hasan (as) therefore achieves his objective of exposing Muawiya as not a good Muslim ruler.
- It now ties Muawiya to govern the Muslim lands (inside and outside Syria) within Islamic rules.
- Does Muawiya keep this part of the agreement? His practices show otherwise; we will highlight ten issues, amongst others, showing he does not do so.
- First, he reduces the amount of the Fitr payment (charity) due on the day of Idd at the end of the fasting month of Ramadhan.
- Second, he removes the Talbiyya recitation from the rituals of Hajj.
- Third, he introduces personal tax which goes into his own personal account; it is reported that when he died, he had about ten million dirhams in his personal account.

- Fourth, he removes the recitation of Quran in court assemblies (gatherings of people for government business) and introduces singing instead.

- Fifth, he introduces lap dancing by girls in the court assemblies.

- Sixth, he has jesters performing in court assemblies; the introduction of singing, dancing and jesters are all aimed at a merry making culture, to distract people from Islamic ways.

- Seventh, he introduces the calling of Adhan before the Idd prayers, contrary to the Prophet's way.

- Eighth, he changes the order of the Idd sermon from being given after the prayers instead of before the prayers.

- Ninth, he purposely wears silk garments, contrary to Islamic law forbidding men to do so.

- Tenth, he distorts Islamic history; he pays people to fabricate and modify original accounts of events in favour of the Umayya family and against the Prophet's Household (Ahlul Bayt); he is so successful at this that until today, Islamic scholars are engaged in distinguishing between authentic and distorted accounts.

Point 2: Muawiya is to take over the political administration; he has no right to pass it on to his successor, but it will return to Imam Hasan (as) on Muawiya's death.

- Imam Hasan (as) hands over temporarily the Political Leadership of the Muslims to Muawiya; this office can be administered by others who do not have to be a Successor (Khalifa) of the Prophet; as was the case for Leader Abu Bakr, Leader Umar and Leader Othman.

- He does not hand over the offices of Spiritual Leadership and Spiritual Authority, as they are divinely appointed; these are not responsibilities to be transferred to others, except by the command of Allah.

- So, there is no abdication of Khalifa as claimed by many historians.

- In fact, Muawiya himself fully understands that he is only offered the political leadership temporarily, for when he speaks to the people of Kufa, he tells them: "I have not fought against you to make you pray, fast, go for Hajj, or pay Zakaat (charity); I have fought to rule over you; this agreement with Imam Hasan (as) is under my foot and I am not bound by them".

- Imam Hasan (as) is younger than Muawiya by twenty two years; so the expectation is that Muawiya would die earlier than Imam Hasan (as), and in that event the political office will return to Imam Hasan (as), as written down in this part of the agreement.

- Does Muawiya keep to this part of the agreement? His practices show otherwise; before his death, he ensures that the political office goes to his son, Yazeed.

  - So, by including this point in the agreement, Imam Hasan (as) achieves his objective of exposing Muawiya as a leader who cannot be trusted to keep his word, despite signing an agreement.

Point 3: All the people of Islamic territories are to be protected.

- Imam Hasan (as) wants to ensure that all people living in the areas controlled by the Muslim government, predominantly in Syria, Iraq and Arabia, are treated equally; he ensures that people of different faiths are not discriminated against in receiving any government services.

- Does Muawiya keep to this part of the agreement? His practices show otherwise; many people, principally in Basra and Kufa (in Iraq), are harassed, tortured and even killed for their political activities, for they are seen as being against his government.

  - By including this in the agreement, Imam Hasan (as) achieves his objective of exposing Muawiya as not being a saviour of the Muslims, as he (Muawiya) claims to the Muslim world, but as a killer of the Muslims.

Point 4: Lives, honour and properties of the Shias of Ali must be safeguarded.

- Imam Hasan (as) now wants to ensure that the followers of Imam Ali (as), in particular, are protected from any wrong doings or discrimination by the government.

- Does Muawiya keep to this part of the agreement? His practices show otherwise.

- In Syria, the Shias are not allowed to work in any branch of the Syrian government: the civil service, judiciary, army, and all other departments.

- In 38 AH (658 AD), Imam Ali (as) appointed Ziyad, who is a talented administrator, to be his governor of Istakhr (near present-day city of Shiraz in Iran); since Ziyad does not side with Muawiya after the death of Imam Ali (as), Muawiya comes up with a plan to win him over.

- Muawiya claims that Ziyad is his half-brother and that it was his father Abu Sufyan who is the father of Ziyad, with a different mother; this is an astonishing claim that puts to shame the honour of Abu Sufyan, and also the honour of Ziyad as an illegitimate child.

- Having established this false blood relationship, Muawiya offers Ziyad the governorship of Basra in 44 AH (664 AD), with the aim of getting Basra to support the rule of Muawiya.

- Ziyad rules Basra with oppression and tyranny and anyone opposing him or Muawiya is killed; Muawiya also makes him the governor of Kufa in 50 AH (670 AD), and Kufa also submits to the rule of Muawiya under the oppressive and tyrannical rule of Ziyad; Ziyad dies in 53 AH (673 AD).

- Any known Shia is exiled to northern Syria or is denied government allowance which was paid to the people, or is allocated lower quality housing, or is not allowed to work in any government department; these measures are very harsh as working for the government is the main source of livelihood for most people.

- Muawiya's rule is targeted at the Shias, contrary to the terms of the peace agreement.

- By including this in the treaty, Imam Hasan (as) achieves his objective of exposing Muawiya's true nature.

Point 5: Muawiya will not, directly or indirectly, harm, threaten or attempt to kill any of the member of the Prophet's family.

- Imam Hasan (as) wants to ensure the peace and security of the Hashimis, the Prophet's family.

- Does Muawiya keep to this part of the agreement? His practices show otherwise.

- He denies the Hashimis many of the government services and benefits that other citizens enjoy; they are allocated low quality housing; the Khums tax money that is due to them is denied.

- By including this in the agreement, Imam Hasan (as) achieves his objective of exposing Muawiya as an enemy of the Prophet and his family, rather than as friend as he is claiming to the public.

- Muawiya in fact successfully plans and finances the killing of Imam Hasan (as); he uses Joda Ashath, a wife of Imam Hasan (as), to put poison in his food in return for money and a promise to be married to his son Yazeed.

- On poisoning and killing Imam Hasan (as), Muawiya pays Joda but does not allow the promised marriage to take place; for he tells her that if she was willing to kill one husband, she could well do it again to his son Yazeed.

  - We again see that Imam Hasan (as) achieves his objective of exposing Muawiya as a murderer, rather than the pious Muslim he portrays himself to be.

Point 6: Muawiya will stop the practice of cursing Imam Ali (as).

- Muawiya started the practice of cursing Imam Ali (as) especially in the Friday prayer sermons; this was going on in the major cities in Syria to start off with; when Muawiya becomes the Leader of the Muslims, he spreads this practice to Iraq and Arabia.

- Does Muawiya keep to this part of the agreement? His practices show otherwise.

- He and subsequent leaders continue with this practice; it is finally stopped after about sixty five years later (35-100 AH, 656-719 AD) by the ruler Leader Umar Abdul Aziz, during the time of the sixth Imam, Imam Jaffer Sadiq (as).

- Imam Hasan (as) achieves his objective of exposing Muawiya for what he is, an arch enemy of Imam Ali (as) and an unprincipled man, contrary to what he is claiming to be.

Fruits of the peace agreement

- The reasons for the peace agreement sought by both parties have been mentioned in Section 4.6 in this chapter.

- The wisdom of Imam Hasan (as) in agreeing to this peace agreement becomes clear then and is everlasting for he exposes Muawiya for what he truly is.

- Muawiya is exposed in such a manner that today, centuries later, **all** scholars and historians from every sect of the Muslim community do not refer to Muawiya as a Rightly Guided Leader; they give only the first four leaders after the Prophet the title of the Rightly Guided Leader.

- Imam Hasan (as) and Muawiya come to Kufa; Muawiya takes the agreement document and tells the people of Kufa the reason for securing an agreement is to purely rule over them and not to guide them in any religious and spiritual aspects; and he says he has no intention of keeping to any part of it once he got the rulership; this explains why he gave Imam

Hasan (as) a blank signed paper to write down the terms of the agreement.

- By the middle of 40 AH (661 AD), about six months after the death of Imam Ali (as), Imam Hasan (as) together with his whole family leave Kufa and return to Madinah.

4.8 Impressions on Imam Husein (as)

- When Imam Hasan (as) dies in 50 AH (670 AD), he is forty six years old; some lasting impressions are left on him of Imam Hasan's (as) ways.

- Let us now examine how they influence the way he deals with the situations leading to Karbala.

- First, he sees that Imam Hasan (as) did not abandon his responsibilities of Spiritual Leadership and Spiritual Authority even when he is not the Political Leader.

- He does exactly the same during his time; when the Political Office is denied to him (by Muawiya and Yazeed), he still carries on with the responsibilities of Spiritual Leadership and Spiritual Authority.

- Second, he sees that Imam Hasan (as) honours the peace agreement, even though the opposite side breaks it on every point.

- After the death of Imam Hasan (as) in 50 AH (670 AD), the people of Kufa write to Imam Husein (as) to become their Political Leader also, but he refuses to do so because he is honouring the agreement made by Imam Hasan (as) and Muawiya that the political office would remain with Muawiya until his death.

- Third, he sees from Imam Hasan (as) that a peace agreement, without compromising on Islamic principles, is to be preferred for the greater cause, and the survival of Islam and avoiding wars.

5 Before Karbala

50 AH - 60 AH
670 AD - 680 AD

In this chapter, we will look at the situation during the ten year period, between the deaths of Imam Hasan (as) and Muawiya. We will see why Imam Husein (as) refuses to pledge his allegiance to Yazeed and the consequences of this decision.

5.1 Muawiya plans for Yazeed's succession

- The time period is 50-60 AH (670-680 AD).
- Muawiya is the Political Leader of the Muslims from 41 AH (661 AD), and calls himself the Commander of the Faithful (Amir-ul-Momineen); the capital city now moves from Kufa to Damascus (in Syria).
- He wants to make his son Yazeed succeeds him as the leader of the Muslims.
- His plan gains momentum when in 50 AH (670 AD) Mughira Shuba approaches Muawiya to offer his support for Yazeed's succession.
- Mughira Shuba is a prominent personality and in the political and ruling class circles of the

time; Muawiya makes him the governor of Kufa from 41 AH (661 AD).

- Later, when Mughira hears that Muawiya wants to replace him as the governor of Kufa, he comes up with a devious plan.
- He says to Muawiya that he should consider making Yazeed his successor and that he (Mughira) would rally support for this plan in Kufa, Ziyad (the governor of Basra) should do the same in Basra, and so should the governors in Arabia (principally Madinah and Makkah) should do the same; there would be no opposition in Syria due to Muawiya's total control there.
- Muawiya likes the idea and therefore does not remove Mughira from the Kufa governorship.
- Muawiya now starts to plan for Yazeed to take over when he dies; he knows he will meet a lot of opposition, mostly from the people of Arabia and Iraq, mainly for two reasons.
- First, Yazeed is known for his bad character and un-Islamic ways.
- Second, he knows of the people's expectation that the next political leader should be chosen by popular choice, and not by personal nomination.

- So, he uses different methods to ensure that Yazeed becomes his successor; this is done over a period of six years from 50-56 AH (670-767 AD).

- He travels to Madinah to gauge the public support for his plan; Madinah is the spiritual city of Islam, and if the elders of Madinah accept the plan, then other provinces like Makkah, Kufa and Basra will follow.

- There he meets up with the elders of the city: Abdullah Abbas, Abdullah Jaffer, Abdullah Zobayr and Abdullah Umar; all of them leave Muawiya in no doubt about their strong opposition to his plan.

- He does not invite Imam Hasan (as) and Imam Husein (as) for he already knows they will never agree to his plan.

- He heads back to Damascus and starts working on his plan.

- First, he decides he has to remove Imam Hasan (as), for he is bound by the peace agreement in that the political leadership would have to return to Imam Hasan (as) on his death.

- Imam Hasan (as) is about twenty years younger than Muawiya, so the expectation is

Muawiya will die first; in this case, the political leadership will return to Imam Hasan (as) and not go to his son Yazeed.

- Therefore, his first plan of action is to get Imam Hasan (as) murdered; he arranges to bribe Joda, a wife of Imam Hasan (as), with money and a promise to get her married to his son Yazeed; Joda poisons Imam Hasan (as) and he dies; Muawiya pays the money to Joda but does not get her married to Yazeed.

- Second, he pays the poets to compose praising and glorifying poems of Yazeed and then recite them in public; the recitation of poetry was a very effective means of communication at the time.

- Third, he pays a lot of money to the influential and prominent people who are resisting his plan.

- Fourth, an order goes out to all the governors in the provinces that they should publicly support the decree from Syria for the nomination of Yazeed.

- Fifth, he organises a conference in Damascus (Syria) where delegations from all the provinces attend; he then tells them of the need and suitability of Yazeed's nomination as his successor; the conference is carefully stage-managed to show full support for

Yazeed; however, some delegations refuse to support his plan.

- Sixth, he comes to Madinah for the second time, the centre of the spirituality of Islam; he sets up a meeting with a handful of prominent people of Madinah (though he excludes Imam Husein (as) from this meeting, for his views against the leadership of Muawiya and his plan to nominate Yazeed are known by all); this group tells Muawiya that they do not support him in his plan.

- Seventh, he stops the public financial benefits to the people, in particular the Hashimis (the Prophet's family), for their opposition to his plan.

- Eighth, he resorts to engineer the murders of the influential people who are opposing his plans (having already engineered the murder of Imam Hasan (as) earlier); people like Saad Waqqas, Abdur Rahman Khalid, Abdur Rahman Abu Bakr and Hujr Al-Kindi are thus all killed.

- Ninth, he comes to Madinah for the third time in 56 AH (676 AD); he calls for a meeting with Imam Husein (as) and Abdullah Abbas (see Chart 4 on page 255) and tries to convince them of the merits of Yazeed (other reports say that Abdullah Zobayr was also present);

Imam Husein (as) explains to him why Yazeed is unsuitable to be the leader of the Muslims and he holds Muawiya responsible for this plan; Muawiya is left in no doubt that Imam Husein (as) will never pledge his allegiance to Yazeed.

- Imam Husein (as) and the other elders leave Madinah for Makkah, for they do not want to be around when Muawiya is there; in the absence of the elders, Muawiya calls up a public meeting and intimidates the people of Madinah into agreeing to his plan.

- Tenth, when Muawiya leaves Madinah for Makkah for the Umrah (the out-of-season pilgrimage), he again meets up with Imam Husein (as) (who is with Abdullah Zobayr and Abdullah Umar - the prominent elders of Madinah); he instructs his guards to escort Imam Husein (as) and his group to the Kabah, with the instruction to kill them if any of them say a word while he is addressing the people.

- He takes to the pulpit and falsely tells the people gathered there that since the elders of Madinah (pointing to Imam Husein (as) and his group) have pledged their allegiance to Yazeed, then the people of Makkah must also do so which they do (Imam Husein (as) did not say anything here to avoid any bloodshed near the Kabah); he immediately heads back to Damascus.

- So we see how Muawiya uses a variety of methods: intimidation, bribery, lies, political manoeuvrings, deceit, intrigue, oppression, withholding of public allowances and even murder to ensure Yazeed is nominated his successor.

What does Imam Husein (as) do?

- When Imam Hasan (as) dies in 50 AH (670 AD), the people of Kufa write to Imam Husein (as) asking him to be their Political Leader; he tells them that he is bound by the peace agreement signed by his brother Imam Hasan (as) (part of which says the political leadership remains with Muawiya until his death; it would then come back to Imam Hasan (as)).

- After 56 AH (676 AD), when Muawiya has secured the allegiance for Yazeed in the provinces, delegations from the provinces come to Imam Husein (as) complaining about the injustices and the oppressive rule of Muawiya.

- When Muawiya hears of these delegations, he writes to Imam Husein (as) to tell him to keep out of such matters for the peace agreement does not permit him to take on the political leadership.

- In his reply, Imam Husein (as) details all that is wrong with his government and policies, and his murderous ways.

- In one of the Hajj seasons, Imam Husein (as) calls for a public meeting where he informs the people of the ways of Muawiya's rule and his long time policy to sideline the Prophet's family.

- Muawiya is clever enough not to pursue the matter any further with Imam Husein (as) and leaves him alone.

- Muawiya dies in Rajjab 60 AH (680 AD).

5.2 Character of Yazeed

- Yazeed was born in 25 AH (645 AD) and is thirty five years old when his father dies.

- He is an alcoholic and is often seen drunk in public.

- He is obsessed with hunting of wild animals; when his father dies, he is out hunting and does not come back for the funeral.

- He flouts the Islamic laws openly.

- He is shameless.
- His morals are very loose.
- He indulges in singing and music.
- He is a gambler.
- He engages in sexual activities with women who are unlawful to him.
- He lacks any protocol, political and administrative experience and wisdom of a leader.

5.3 Allegiance – Yazeed demands

- Just before his death, Muawiya leaves a will for his son Yazeed telling him that the allegiance for his leadership has been secured from all the provinces, but for three people in Madinah – Imam Husein (as), Abdullah Umar and Abdullah Zobayr.
- He tells him that Abdullah Umar and Abdullah Zobayr should not pose any problems; however, he should treat Imam Husein (as) with care for the people of Iraq will rally behind him to oppose his leadership.

- On coming to office, despite the advice of his father to handle the rulership with care, Yazeed immediately forces a confrontation by issuing his first decree that the three individuals in Madinah must swear allegiance to him and recognise him as Commander of the Faithful (Amir-ul-Momineen).

- An order is sent to Walid Utba, the governor of Madinah, a cousin of Yazeed (see Chart 5 on page 257); he orders them to get a pledge of allegiance from the three people (Imam Husein (as), Abdullah Umar and Abdullah Zobayr) and to give them no choice in this matter.

- It is worth noting here that Muawiya, who was an experienced politician and tactician, never demanded a personal oath of allegiance from Imam Husein (as); Yazeed, with no such experience and wisdom, crudely forces this issue against the advice of his father.

- Walid sends for Imam Husein (as), Abdullah Umar and Abdullah Zobayr; it is Friday, 26 Rajjab, 60 AH (May, 680 AD).

- As for Abdullah Umar, some reports say he was in Madinah and comes to meet Walid where he says he will pledge his allegiance once everyone else does; he is let go for the authorities do not regard him as a threat to Yazeed; other reports say he was out of

Madinah at the time and on his return, meets Walid and pledges his allegiance.

- As for Abdullah Zobayr, he is with Imam Husein (as) in the Prophet's mosque when the order from Walid comes through; he refuses to go to Walid at the governor's palace; he leaves for Makkah with his brother on the same night, Friday, the eve of 27 Rajjab 60 AH; he avoids taking the main road to Makkah but takes the inside roads to avoid detection by the authorities.

- The next day, when the authorities in Madinah find out he has left the previous night, they send a search party through the main road to Makkah, but are not able to track him; they do not pursue the matter for they do not regard him as a threat.

- As for Imam Husein (as), he goes to meet Walid at the governor's palace.

- Yazeed insists on a personal allegiance from Imam Husein (as); even though all the people in Syria, Iraq and Arabia, through their leaders, have pledged their allegiance, he is aware of their reservations and that the allegiances have come under duress and extracted by his father, Muawiya.

- He recognises that the personal allegiance from Imam Husein (as) will give his political leadership legitimacy, recognition, stature, credibility and endorsement; for if it is good enough for Imam Husein (as), then it must be good enough for all the rest of the Muslims.

- If Imam Husein (as) were to approve the leadership of Yazeed, then there will be no objection from anyone that he (Yazeed) is not suitable for the office.

5.4 Allegiance – Imam Husein (as) refuses

- On one side we have the infallible personality of Imam Husein (as), the second grand-son of the Prophet, the son of Imam Ali (as) and Lady Fatema (as), and on the other we have the personification of evil in Yazeed.

- There is simply no way that Imam Husein (as) would even consider the slightest possibility of pledging his allegiance to legitimise the rule of Yazeed.

- When Walid sends for Imam Husein (as), the messenger finds Imam Husein (as) and Abdullah Zobayr in the Prophet's mosque; both confer about the reason for the meeting.

- Imam Husein (as) suspects that Walid wants to break the news of Muawiya's death and ask them to pledge allegiance to Yazeed; Abdullah Zobayr decides not to go for the meeting and he leaves the city for Makkah on the same night in secret.

- Imam Husein (as) goes to meet Walid; he takes with him the youths from his family, in case of any confrontation, and tells them to wait outside the room; they are to come to his aid if they hear him talking in a raised voice.

- Walid meets with Imam Husein (as); Marwan Hakam (see Chart 5 on page 257) is also present at the meeting; he is the previous governor of Madinah and the legal adviser and counsellor for the Umayyas.

- Walid informs Imam Husein (as) of the death of Muawiya and the order he received from Yazeed to obtain his pledge of allegiance to Yazeed or to kill him.

- Imam Husein (as) has now two choices; either gives his pledge of allegiance, which as we said earlier, is not even a remote possibility to be considered; the alternative is to stand up to Yazeed which he knew would lead eventually to his martyrdom.

- It is clear to Imam Husein (as) that death is the price he has to pay; so the only consideration is to make his death an effective weapon for opposition to Yazeed; death in the governor's palace or in Madinah would be very quickly hushed up by the authorities who would make him appear as a rebel.

- This strategy to make an effective opposition to Yazeed begins to take shape, right in the governor's palace; he tells Walid that surely an important matter like getting an allegiance from him should not be done in private amongst a few people, but must be done in public when he informs them of this important news; Walid agrees and lets Imam Husein (as) go and asks him to attend the public gathering when it is arranged.

- Marwan, who is also present at this meeting, advises Walid against this; he tells him that if Imam Husein (as) is let free now without giving his allegiance, then he will never be able to get it later on; so it is better to force his allegiance now or kill him; Walid refuses to do this out of respect for Imam Husein (as).

- Imam Husein (as) challenges both of them to kill him there and then if they were brave enough; he then walks out and together with the youths goes back to his house.

5.5 Strategies of Imam Husein (as)

- It is now Friday night, the eve of 27 Rajjab 60 AH (May 680 AD).

- People of Madinah notice that Imam Husein (as) is in a sombre and thoughtful mood and he spends a lot of time by the graves of the Prophet, his mother Lady Fatema (as) and his brother Imam Hasan (as).

- His mind is occupied planning his strategies, for he knows the authorities will be back the next day to ask for his decision (of allegiance to Yazeed); he has now got the strategies planned out.

- The next day, the authorities are busy tracing Abdullah Zobayr (who left for Makkah the night before), and leave Imam Husein (as) alone for a while.

- Meanwhile, Marwan meets up with Imam Husein (as) during the day; he asks him for his decision; Imam Husein (as) gives him the famous answer: "The likes of me will never pledge allegiance to the likes of Yazeed".

- Imam Husein's (as) decision is now public knowledge.

- This puts Walid in a bit of an awkward position, for if he calls a public meeting, Imam Husein (as) will refuse to pledge his allegiance and this will force him to kill him (as instructed by Yazeed - either the allegiance or the death of Imam Husein (as)); he does not wish to be a party to the killing of Imam Husein (as).

- In the evening he sends his men again to Imam Husein (as) in the last hope that he agree to pledge allegiance and thereby avoid any bloodshed.

- As Walid has been very sympathetic to Imam Husein (as), Imam Husein (as) repays his kindness by showing him a way out of his predicament saying that both parties should reflect over the night; the same night, Imam Husein (as) leaves Madinah for Makkah, thereby relieving Walid of carrying out the order to kill him.

- When Marwan informs Yazeed of Walid's lenient behaviour to Imam Husein (as), Yazeed removes Walid from the office of governor and gives it to Amr Saeed, in addition to being the governor of Makkah at the time.

First strategy

- The first strategy of Imam Husein (as) is to leave his birth city of Madinah for Makkah; there are two main reasons for this.

- First, by remaining in Madinah, the news of his refusal to pledge allegiance will be confined only locally; his strategy is to publicise his opposition to the widest possible audience in the region and not to make it a silent opposition, soon to be forgotten.

- Second, by remaining and being killed in Madinah, the authorities can use the media it controls to spin the killing as simply a rebellion against the government; thus his principled opposition to pledging allegiance to Yazeed would be hidden.

Second strategy

- The second strategy of Imam Husein (as) is to engage in a battle of conscience and not in a military might; the Syrian and its provincial armies are the most powerful in the region, and there will be no victory fighting their military might, however strong an army that Imam Husein (as) may be able to recruit.

- He wants to awaken the slumber, the indifference and the conscience of the people by offering his martyrdom together with his closest family members; this way, he hopes to expose Yazeed as being thoroughly unsuitable as the political leader of the Muslims; hence the decision to take his closest male family members with him on the journey.

Third strategy

- The third strategy of Imam Husein (as) is to ensure that the objectives of his sacrifice do not go unnoticed, and get covered up or distorted by the authorities who control the media of the time.

- He therefore decides to take the women family members who are not obliged to engage in any battle, for the sole purpose that they become his media, in exposing the truth of whatever transpires.

- He tells his family of his decision to leave Madinah; he takes with him a number of his closest male and female family members (see Chart 1 on the inside back cover), including the youngest one month old baby boy (Ali Asghar).

- He leaves behind his daughter, Fatema Sughra, as she is too ill for the journey.

- He leaves behind his brother, Muhammad (Hanafiyya), with the prime responsibility of sending news to Imam Husein (as) about the political developments in Madinah and Syria.

- The news is now spreading in Madinah that Imam Husein (as) and his family are leaving for Makkah; people are now asking the reason for this sudden departure; his objective begins to be achieved.

Fourth strategy

- Having decided to leave Madinah, Imam Husein (as) has a choice to go to any other place in the region.
- However, he chooses Makkah for a particular reason; Makkah is the city where people from all over the region come to perform the Umrah (the out-of-season pilgrimage) and the Hajj (the in-season pilgrimage).
- So, he can get the maximum publicity for his cause in Makkah, and not in any other place.

5.6 Is Imam Husein (as) committing suicide?

- A question that is often posed is this: if Imam Husein (as) knows he cannot face the might of Yazeed's army, is he then not committing suicide by going ahead with his strategies?
- He is fully aware what the consequences of his opposition to Yazeed's ways and his rulership are going to be to himself and to his family; he

has chosen this path after careful consideration, for the alternative is the total corruption of Islamic ways under the rule of Yazeed.

- It is going to take the stature, the charisma, and the infallible personality of Imam Husein (as) to rise up to this challenge.
- Imam Husein's (as) death cannot be considered as a suicide, for if that was his intention, he had five instances where he could have done so.
- First, he could have remained in Madinah, for Yazeed's people would have surely killed him there and then.
- Second, he could have remained in Makkah, instead of moving on from there (as we shall see in Chapter 8), and allow himself to be killed by Yazeed's assassins who come after him.
- Third, he could have walked into the hands of Ubaydullah's security forces who were blocking the southern entry into Kufa, resulting in his arrest and killing; he chose instead to try entering Kufa from the western side which was a more dangerous route because of its hilly ground.

- Fourth, he would not have looked for some peaceful ways to find a way out of the crisis in Karbala (as we shall see in Chapter 8).

- Fifth, he and his family could have offered no resistance in the battlefield in Karbala and simply submitted themselves to be killed; he and his family fought valiantly to their deaths in the battlefield.

- So we see that even with his divine foresight of the tribulations and calamities that he, his family and his companions will face, he embarks on the journey with one purpose in mind - not to commit suicide, but to make a **sacrifice**.

- This is a selfless sacrifice of the supreme and of the purest level, where the motive is simply to save the practices and the pure ways of Islam, as taught by the Prophet - a call to the people to enjoin them to do good actions and refrain from bad ones.

- The alternative is to leave that Islam in a real and imminent danger of being diluted, contaminated, corrupted, crushed and obliterated by the leadership of Yazeed.

5.7 Madinah to Makkah

- It is Saturday night, the eve of 28 Rajjab (May 680 AD); Imam Husein (as) and his selected family are leaving Madinah for Makkah.
- He takes the main road, for he is not trying to hide his movements from the authorities.
- The distance of about two hundred and ten miles is covered in five days.
- He and his family arrive in Makkah on Thursday, 3 Shaban 60 AH (May, 680 AD).
- He arrives in Makkah exactly on his fifty sixth birthday (born on 3 Shaban 4 AH).
- His arrival in Makkah at this time of the year generates more publicity for his cause, since the Hajj (in-season pilgrimage) is five months away.
- People who are in Makkah for the Umrah (the out-of-season pilgrimage) and for the holy fasting month of Ramadhan are asking him the reason for his presence; the intended choice of Makkah as the centre for his publicity campaign is already taking shape.
- It turns out that he is to remain in Makkah for about four months before he leaves the city; during this time, more and more people come to know of his mission.

6 Activities in Kufa

In this chapter, we will look at the activities in Kufa whilst Imam Husein (as) is in Makkah. We will see how these activities have a direct effect on the events leading to Karbala.

6.1 Invitations from the Shias of Kufa

- When Imam Hasan (as) died in 50 AH (670 AD), the Shias (followers of the Prophet's Household - Ahlul Bayt) of Kufa (in Iraq) wrote to Imam Husein (as) to become their Political Leader and rise against the rule of Muawiya; Imam Husein (as) refuses saying he is bound by the peace agreement (between Imam Hasan (as) and Muawiya) that the political leadership is to remain with Muawiya until his death.

- Now, ten years on, in 60 AH (680 AD), the Shias of Kufa come to know that Imam Husein (as) has moved to Makkah and is not pledging his allegiance to Yazeed.

- They come together and agree to invite Imam Husein (as) to come to Kufa; the group is led by Sulayman Surd Khuzai.

- The people are enthusiastic in their support to invite Imam Husein (as) to come to Kufa, and be their Political Leader (in addition to being their Spiritual Leader and Spiritual Authority, that is being their Khalifa).

- They plan to remove the present governor of Kufa, Noman Bashir, and have Imam Husein (as) as their leader, and to use Kufa as the base for opposing Yazeed.

- Sulayman cautions the people that they should consider seriously the question of inviting Imam Husein (as), as this will bring them into direct conflict with Yazeed and the might of the Syrian power.

- They reply that they are ready to face any consequences, even if it means laying down their lives for Imam Husein (as).

- So, the first letter of invitation is signed by the leaders of the group: Sulayman Surd Khuzai, Musayyaba Nokhaba, Rufaa Shadad and Habib Mazaher.

- It is delivered by two messengers, Abdullah Musma and Abdullah Walin, and it reaches Imam Husein (as) in Makkah on 10 Ramadhan 60 AH (14 June 680 AD).

- After two days (12 Ramadhan), Imam Husein (as) receives about one hundred and fifty more letters of invitations from the people of Kufa; these are brought by four messengers: Qays Mushir, Umara Abdullah, and two brothers, Abdullah Shadad and Abd-Rahman Shadad.

- After another two days (14 Ramadhan), another batch of letters of invitations come; the two messengers are Hani Hani and Saeed Abdullah.

6.2 Remain in Makkah or go to Kufa?

- By the middle of the month of Ramadhan, Imam Husein (as) has received a number of letters of invitations from the Shias of Kufa.

- He now has to decide his next step; he either remains in Makkah or goes to Kufa.

- He comes to a double decision; first, he must remain in Makkah for the next three months until the Hajj period when the pilgrims will be arriving in large numbers, and he will get the maximum audience to explain his resistance to pledging allegiance to Yazeed (as this is the reason for his coming to Makkah).

- Second, he is fully aware of how, in the past, the people of Kufa turned against his father,

Imam Ali (as), and his brother, Imam Hasan (as), in their times of need; yet, he is morally bound to answer their call to go there and be their Khalifa.

- So, he takes a precautionary step; he decides to send an ambassador to Kufa to assess first-hand the situation first-hand on the ground there, and to report back to him exactly how solid (or otherwise) the support is for him to go to Kufa.

Ambassador

- The person chosen as his ambassador has to have the best qualities and be the best candidate for this mission.

- His ambassador must have the following qualifications:

  - he must understand fully his mission
  - he is aware completely of the history and politics of Kufa
  - he is very familiar with the tribal loyalties in Kufa
  - he should have his total confidence
  - his judgement has to be trusted by him unequivocally
  - he must command the respect of the people of Kufa
  - he musty be accepted unconditionally by the people of Kufa as his ambassador

- Imam Husein (as) chooses Muslim Aqil as the best candidate.
- He is his first cousin for their fathers, Imam Ali (as) and Aqil, arte brothers (see Chart 6 on page 259).
- In addition, he also his brother-in-law.
- After the death of Lady Fatemah (as), Imam Ali (as) married Lady Umme Habiba and their daughter, Ruqayya, is married to Muslim (see Chart 6 on page 259).
- Imam Husein (as) writes a letter to the people of Kufa; he acknowledges their invitations and tells them he is sending Muslim Aqil as his ambassador to assess the situation and report back to him.
- This letter is taken by the last two messengers who came from Kufa, Hani Hani and Saeed Abdullah.

6.3 Muslim Aqil in Kufa

- As Muslim Aqil is a renowned warrior, Imam Husein (as) tells Muslim to take with him his two youngest sons, Ibraheem and Muhammad, who are both under the age of twelve years, so as to show the peaceful intentions of his mission; the other two children, Abdullah and Muhammad remain with Imam Husein (as) in Makkah.

- The four messengers from Kufa (Qays Mushir, Umara Abdullah, Abdullah Shadad and Abd-Rahman Shadad) accompany Muslim to show him the quickest route to Kufa.

- He leaves Makkah on 15 Ramadhan 60 AH (19 June 680 AD) and goes first to Madinah to brief Muhammad Hanafiyya (Imam Husein's (as) brother) on the latest developments.

- He also gets the news from him that Walid Utba (who sent for Imam Husein (as) upon the orders of Yazeed) has been replaced as the governor, that Madinah is quiet and there has been no mobilisation of the Syrian army.

- He now leaves Madinah with two more local guides, his two children and the four messengers from Kufa; nine people are now on their way to Kufa.

- During the journey, the two local guides fall ill and before they died, they were able to show him the right direction to Kufa.

- About halfway between Madinah and Kufa, at a place called Madiq, Muslim writes a letter to Imam Husein (as) informing him of the progress of his journey so far; the letter is taken by one of the messengers, Qays Mushir.

- Muslim and his small group arrive in Kufa on 5 Shawwal 60 AH (8 July 680 AD), nineteen days after leaving Makkah.

- He and his two children put up at the house of Mukhtar Thaqafee who is one of the chiefs of the tribes and is a dedicated and loyal follower of the Prophet's Household.

- Muslim meets with the local leaders of the Shias (followers of the Prophet's Household) to gauge the extent of the support for Imam Husein (as); some of the leaders are Sulayman Khuzai, Mukhtar Thaqafee, Muslim Awsaja, Habib Mazaher, Musayyaba Nokhaba and Rufaa Shadad.

- Muslim and his deputies (the local Shia leaders) are actively rallying support for Imam Husein (as) from the people of Kufa; this goes on for about two months in Shawwal and Zilkad 60 AH (July/August 680 AD).

- About eighteen thousand people pledge their support for Imam Husein (as) at the end of this period.

6.4 Who are these supporters?

- Such a large number of supporters raises the question if they are really all genuinely committed to support the cause of Imam Husein (as).

- There are three groups of supporters.

- The first group are the true and loyal supporters of the Prophet's Household; they are genuine in their invitation to Imam Husein (as), and are ready to support him whatever the circumstances and the difficulties they might face from the authorities in Kufa.

- The second group are people who are not happy to be under the control of Yazeed in Damascus; they see Imam Husein (as) as a credible person who can help them remove Yazeed's governor in Kufa.

- The third group are the mercenaries; they are supporting Imam Husein (as) purely for their own material gain and to benefit from the booty and spoils of war.

- Muslim is well aware of the composition of these three groups; he makes the judgement that, even allowing for their different motives and for some people withdrawing their support when the time comes, Imam Husein (as) will have enough support, first to remove

Yazeed's governor (Noman Bashir) from Kufa and then make Kufa the base to oppose Yazeed's un-Islamic rule.

- Around the middle of Zilkad 60 AH (mid August 680 AD), he writes a letter to Imam Husein (as) telling him to leave Makkah and to come to Kufa where there is a large number of people waiting and ready to support him in his mission.

6.5 Change of governors

- When Muslim is in Kufa, the governor of Yazeed is Noman Bashir.

- Muslim and his deputies are openly rallying support for Imam Husein (as) and all know that he is staying at Mukhtar's house.

- Noman is also aware of Muslim's activities and has full knowledge of what is going on in Kufa.

- Civil servants in Kufa who are supporters of Yazeed, tell Noman to take action against Muslim, or else he will be thrown out of office by the supporters of Muslim if he is allowed to continue with his activities.

- Noman refuses to do so; he informs them that he is not going to arrest Muslim or his supporters for until now, they have not broken any laws.

- He warns Muslim and his supporters that should they start a revolution against him and his government, then he will arrest and imprison them.

- On realising that Noman is not taking any action against Muslim, the civil servants write a letter to Yazeed in Damascus.

- In the letter (which is sent at about the same time as Muslim sends his letter to Imam Husein (as)), they inform Yazeed of Muslim's activities, the impending danger if Imam Husein (as) comes to Kufa and the reluctance of Noman to put a stop to these activities.

- Yazeed is at a loss as to what he should do to stop losing control of Kufa.

- He consults Sarjun, the government adviser (he was also an adviser to Muawiya - Yazeed's father).

- Sarjun tells him that he should do exactly what his father had done when he realised that Basra was in danger of going out of his control; he sent Ziyad as a governor to crush all resistance and impose a strict and oppressive rule on the followers of the Prophet's Household.

- Sarjun advises Yazeed to send Ubaydullah, the son of Ziyad (who was the governor of Kufa as well as Basra in Muawiya's time), to Kufa to replace Noman as the governor; Ubaydullah is the governor of Basra since 55 AH (676 AD), and he is now (in 60 AH - 680 AD) going to be the governor of Kufa as well as Basra.

- Ubaydullah, like his father Ziyad, is known for his oppressive and dictatorial rule in Basra; the idea is for him to repeat this in Kufa so that there is no more opposition to Yazeed's government there.

- Yazeed sends an order to Ubaydullah that in addition to being the governor of Basra, he should go to Kufa, replace Noman as the governor, put an end to the activities of Muslim, and not allow Imam Husein (as) to enter Kufa.

- Ubaydullah calls a public meeting in Basra; he tells the people that Yazeed has asked him to go to Kufa for an important work, but he does not give them the details; he leaves his brother Othman in charge whilst he is away.

- He gives them a severe warning that should anyone try to destabilise his rule in his absence, then they would be severely dealt with and executed with their families; people take this warning seriously for Ubaydullah has a history of an oppressive rule in Basra.

- He takes his entourage with him and they leave for Kufa; he wants to make an unannounced entry for two reasons.

- First, he wants to find out first-hand the level of support that Muslim Aqil has rallied for Imam Husein (as).

- Second, he fears that the people of Kufa may not let him in if they know of his arrival; for they would still remember the tyranny and the atrocities committed by his father Ziyad when he was the governor of Kufa.

- He comes up with the following plan; he arrives on the outskirts of Kufa at dusk when people cannot see his face clearly; he puts on a black turban; he covers his face with a piece of cloth (this is normal for desert travellers to shield from the sand storms).

- He then instructs his entourage that on entering Kufa and while riding through the streets they should surround him shouting "Welcome Imam".

- As he rides from one district to another in Kufa, the locals come out into the streets thinking that this is Imam Husein (as); for the person is wearing a black turban like the one of Imam Husein (as), his face is not visible for it is dark and it is partially covered with a piece of cloth, and they hear shouts of "Welcome Imam".

- A huge crowd follows him to the city centre and people are joyful for they think that Imam Husein (as) has at last come to them.

- He sees for himself the huge support for Imam Husein (as) and how successful Muslim Aqil has been in gathering this support.

- He heads straight for the governor's palace, near the central mosque and calls Noman Bashir, the governor of Kufa.

- Noman thinks it is Imam Husein (as) calling him, for he has got the news that he has come to Kufa; Noman tells him that he should not cause any problems for his government, or he would have no choice but to arrest him.

- Ubaydullah now removes the turban, the face cloth and tells Noman that by the order of Yazeed, he is removed as the governor of Kufa and Ubaydullah takes over as the new governor.

6.6 Manhunt for Muslim Aqil

- The following day in the morning, Ubaydullah holds a meeting with his security forces in his palace.

- He gives orders that all the tribal chiefs must keep a close watch on their people; they are to report to the security forces anyone who is any way associated with Muslim Aqil; failure to do so means that they will charged with treason, punishable by imprisonment or execution.

- People realise that this is not just a scare tactic, for they are aware of his tyranny in Basra and also of his late father's tyranny in Kufa itself.

- The army and the security forces are put on full alert to ensure that there are no public meetings and that Muslim Aqil is tracked down and arrested.

- As people know where Muslim and his children are staying and that an order has now been issued for his arrest, he therefore moves houses.

- He moves his two children, Muhammad and Ibraheem, from the house of Mukhtar Thaqafee to another safe house; he also moves to the house of another loyal supporter, Hani Urwa; this move is kept very secret and only the selected few know about this.

- The security forces are finding it difficult to track down Muslim; so Ubaydullah uses an experienced spy, called Moaqqal, and gives him three thousand dirhams to use to infiltrate Muslim's network and to gather information about Muslim's hiding place and plans.

- Muslim Awsaja is the intermediary between the people and Muslim Aqil; Moaqqal sees that people usually gather around him in the mosque; so he approaches him with a story that he has run away from Damascus to escape from the persecution of Yazeed; he wants to support Muslim Aqil and has brought some money that he wants to contribute towards his cause.

- After a few meetings with Muslim Awsaja, who gets taken in by his stories, Moaqqal tells him that he wants to meet Muslim Aqil in person to hand over the money to him.

- Moaqqal meets Muslim Aqil in Hani Urwa's house; he comes to see him a number of times, each time meeting the other supporters and gathering information about their plans.

- Moaqqal now knows of Muslim's network and he reports his finding back to Ubaydullah; Muslim and his network are now compromised.

- Ubaydullah has regular meetings with the tribal chiefs; Hani Urwa has not been attending them for fear of being forced to reveal information about Muslim.

- He sends for Hani to come to the governor's palace where he is questioned about the whereabouts of Muslim; Hani denies all knowledge of him in trying to protect him.

- He then calls in Moaqqal; Hani realises that Moaqqal has betrayed him and is a spy for Ubaydullah.

- Ubaydullah tells Hani to send word to Muslim to come to the palace voluntarily; Hani refuses to do so as he does not want to betray him.

- Hani is beaten up and is locked up in the dungeon in the palace.

- When the tribe of Hani hears of his arrest and the rumour that he has been murdered, they get together and come to the governor's palace to seek revenge on his killer.

- When Ubaydullah realises the danger, he asks Shurayh, the Judge of Kufa, whose word the people of Hani would believe, to go the dungeon and verify for himself that Hani is alive; he sees that Hani is alive but bruised and he has a talk with Hani; when he reports this to his group outside, they then disperse.

- At the same time, when Muslim hears of Hani's arrest, he calls upon his supporters to come out in the streets and march to the governor's palace to get Hani released and remove Ubaydullah from office.

- Of about eighteen thousand who pledged their support, around four thousand only come out; there are reasons for this lower figure.

- First, this is a sudden unplanned mobilisation of people and many are unaware of it.

- Second, Kufa is a city made up of distinct localities, with one main road between the districts; hence word had to be sent around to various districts very quickly; in no time, these main roads are now patrolled by the security forces who stop people from getting onto the streets.

- Third, some people are already arrested and are in custody.

- It is worth noting that the main supporters like Sulayman Khuzai, Mosayyaba Nokhaba, Rufaa

Shadad and Muslim Awsaja are not able to join Muslim for one of the three reasons above.

- The day is 8 Zilhajj 60 AH (9 September 680 AD); Muslim with about four thousand supporters march towards the city centre to the governor's palace.

- When Ubaydullah gets the news that Muslim and his supporters are coming to the palace, he goes to the central mosque next door; from there he issues a stern warning to the tribal chiefs (who are with him to warn their people not to join together with Muslim; those who have joined in should return to their homes immediately.

- Ubaydullah then goes back to the palace, calls the tribal chiefs and uses them as human shields, in the hope that the people outside who may force their way in the palace to attack him will not do so for fear of hurting their chiefs in the process.

- He then uses three tactics to persuade people to desert Muslim Aqil and return to their homes.

- First, he calls two of his army officers who are in charge of the manhunt - Muhammad Ashath (bother of Joda Ashath, who killed Imam Hasan (as), and the father of Ashath Qays (who gave Imam Ali (as) a lot of trouble) and Haseen Nameer, the chief of police of Kufa.

- He tells them to go out and spread the word around that a huge army from Damascus is approaching Kufa, and that the supporters of Muslim should abandon him rather than face the onslaught of the Syrian army.

- It was not true that the Syrian army was on its way, but many of the supporters get frightened by the prospect of fighting with the powerful Syrian army and therefore decide to abandon Muslim and return to their homes.

- Second, Ubaydullah tells the tribal chiefs to go around telling their people that their regular government allowance and housing will be withdrawn if they continue to support Muslim.

- When the womenfolk of Muslim's supporters hear of this, they come out and plead with their men to abandon Muslim and return home; they tell the men that this is not their fight and they should not risk their lives and homes for a cause that is not of direct concern to them; so more people abandon Muslim.

- Third, Ubaydullah offers Muslim's supporters an immediate amnesty and a promise of no further investigations, detention or execution should they abandon Muslim now - people are in no doubt of the persecution to follow if Ubaydullah is still in power; even more people abandon Muslim and return to their homes.

- Ubaydullah is so successful in his tactics that from about four thousand people who joined Muslim at the start of the day, only about thirty remain with him by evening time.

- When Muslim comes of the central mosque for the evening prayers, there were ten only; while walking in the streets, they also desert him.

- It must be noted that the loyal supporters were not able to join Muslim due to the sudden unplanned mobilisation of the people; the people who abandoned Muslim were of that group who had their own motives as discussed in Section 6.4.

6.7 Martyrdom of Muslim Aqil

- Night has set in; a curfew is in place, it is now the eve of 9 Zilhajj 60 AH (9 September 680 AD); Muslim is alone, abandoned by his so-called supporters.

- Ubaydullah orders three directives to catch Muslim Aqil.

- First, he orders Haseen Nameer, the chief of police of Kufa and a military officer to seal the border around Kufa immediately.

- Second, he wants a house-to-house search to be conducted in the early morning.

- Third, he offers a reward to anyone who provides information leading to the arrest of Muslim.

- Meanwhile, as Muslim walks down the street, he finds himself in the district belonging to the tribe of Kinda and populated by the family of Jabala; he knocks on one of the doors of a house; a lady by the name of Tawwa answers and asks for some water.

- She is surprised to see that a lone person in the night when a curfew is in place; so she asks him if he is aware of the curfew as the security forces are looking for Muslim Aqil.

- Muslim tells her that he is the one who is being tracked down; Tawwa has respect for the Prophet's Household, so she lets him in; she puts him up in a guest room and gives him some food.

- Tawwa has a son by the name of Bilal; when he comes home, he realises that there is someone in the house; the mother at first refuses to reveal his identity to Bilal for fear that her son would report him to the security forces; he finally finds out that he is the man wanted by Ubaydullah.

- Bilal decides to claim the reward by giving the information to the security forces.

- Early next morning, he informs Abd Rahman, the son of Muhammad Ashath (one of the government army officers put in charge to look for Muslim) where Muslim is.

- Abd Rahman informs his father and he in turn informs Ubaydullah who orders the capture of Muslim, dead or alive.

- Muhammad Ashath takes a unit of about seventy armed soldiers and surrounds the house of Tawwa; Muslim does not want any harm to come to Tawwa, so he comes out of the house with his sword drawn.

- The soldiers make a plan to trap Muslim; they dig a trench in one of the streets and conceal it; some soldiers climb on roofs of the houses along the street and throw fire bombs and stones at Muslim; as he fights his way through, he falls into the concealed trench, badly wounded.

- Muhammad Ashath gives him a guarantee of security, so Muslim gives himself up.

- Muslim asks Muhammad Ashath to send a message to Imam Husein (as) no to come to Kufa as the situation has changed completely; Muhammad Ashath replies that he will do so.

- Muslim is brought before Ubaydullah and his military officers, amongst whom were Umar Saad, Shimr Ziljawshan, Haseen Nameer, Khooli, Sinan and Muhammad Ashath.

- Ubaydullah charges Muslim with treason and orders that he should be taken to the roof and beheaded.

- Muslim asks for some last wishes to be honoured after his death (a verbal will); Ubaydullah nominates Umar Saad to hear the wishes, as he is a distant relation to Muslim; Umar Saad takes him to the side to hear his wishes in private; he has three wishes.

- The first is that the armoury and the sword of his should be sold and the money used to pay off his debt to some people in Kufa.

- The second is that a letter should be sent to Imam Husein (as) in Makkah to inform him not to come to Kufa anymore as the situation has changed completely.

- The third is that his body should be given a proper burial.

- Umar Saad then relates these wishes to Ubaydullah; Ubaydullah tells Muslim that his armoury will be sold to pay off his debts, he has no inertest in what happens to his body after his execution, and that the government will not harm Imam Husein (as) if he is not coming to Kufa and cause problems for his government (literature shows that a letter written earlier by Muhammad Ashath is sent to Imam Husein (as) telling him not to come to Kufa).

- Muslim is taken to the roof of the building, made to position his head over the roof wall and is beheaded by Bakr Humra al-Ahmari; the head falls to the ground, and his body is also thrown to the ground.

- It is then dragged along the streets of Kufa to the market square of the city (city centre) where it is crucified to a wall, as a warning to the people of Kufa not to revolt against the government or support Imam Husein (as).

- Muslim Aqil is the first martyr linked to the tragedy of Karbala (martyred on 9 Zilhajj 60 AH, 10 September 680 AD)

- Hani Urwa (a loyal supporter of Muslim and in whose house Muslim was staying after Ubaydullah came to Kufa) is taken to the market square and is beheaded.

- Ubaydullah orders that the heads of these two martyrs should be sent to Yazeed in Damascus.

- Muslim's two sons, Muhammad and Ibraheem, are also killed in Kufa about one year later.

7 To Karbala

In this chapter, we will trace the route taken by Imam Husein (as) from Makkah to Karbala. We will describe what happens at the stopping points between these two places.

Refer to Chart 7 on page 261. Note that:

- the map is not drawn to scale
- the distances between the places is not known
- most of these places no longer exist by these names
- the exact location of most of these places are not known
- what is shown is a trend in their relative directions

7.1 Makkah

☪ Imam Husein (as) and some of his family left Madinah on 28 Rajjab 60 (May, 680 AD) and arrived in Makkah on 3 Shaban 60 AH (May, 680 AD); the journey of about two hundred and ten miles was covered in five days.

☪ Abdullah Abbas, son of the Prophet's uncle (see Chart 4 on page 255), who lives in Makkah, advises Imam Husein (as) not to go to Kufa for out of fear for his safety.

- When he fails to persuade him, he tells him not to take the women and children with him; Imam Husein (as) tells him that he is taking them for a purpose (as explained in Section 5.5).

- Some reports indicate that Imam Husein's (as) brother, Muhammad Hanafiyya, comes from Madinah to give him the same advise; Imam Husein (as) gives him the same reply as he gave to Abdullah Abbas.

- Whilst Imam Husein (as) is in Makkah, Yazeed sends assassins disguised as pilgrims to assassinate him.

- The assassins are in Makkah by 8 Zilhajj 60 AH (9 September 680 AD), a day before the Day of Arafat (the day when pilgrims go for supplication to the plains of Arafat, about fifteen miles from Makkah) in the Hajj rituals.

- When Imam Husein (as) gets to know about this, his first consideration is to preserve the sanctity of the Kabah and to ensure that there should be no bloodshed in the vicinity of the Kabah and in the holy city of Makkah.

- So he changes his intention from performing the in-season pilgrimage of Hajj to an out-of-season pilgrimage of Umrah and completes the rituals.

- He then tells his family that they should leave Makkah immediately and go to Kufa.

- This sudden departure in itself generates more publicity for Imam Husein's (as) cause; for people are asking why the grand-son of the Holy Prophet is leaving Makkah just hours before the Hajj rituals begin.

- A group of supporters, about one hundred (inferred estimate from the number of martyrs in Karbala and those who join him on the way and at Karbala), also join him.

- The first leg of the journey begins on 8 Zilhajj 60 AH (9 September 680 AD), and the group leaves Makkah and heads towards Kufa.

- Coincidentally, this is the same day that Muslim Aqil and his supporters gather to confront Ubaydullah, the governor of Kufa.

- It is a long journey (about eight hundred miles) through the desert, and there are various stopping places along the way.

- Some of these stops are just resting points; some are small villages; some are oasis in the desert, where food and water supplies are replenished.

- We will only highlight the stopping places which are of historical interest.

7.2 Tanim and Saffah

Tanim

- This is a large and busy resting/stopping point where traders break their journeys.
- Today, it is one of the Miqat points - a place where pilgrims put on their Hajj uniform (Ehram) enter the city boundary of Makkah.
- Imam Husein (as) meets up with a group of traders from Syria who are on their way to Yemen.
- Imam Husein (as) had to leave the city of Makkah in a hurry, and had no time to stock up for the long journey ahead.
- Imam Husein (as) buys a stock of supplies from these traders for the journey ahead - camels, horses, tents, food, water bottles (made of animal skins), and clothes.
- The inference is that he also buys from them any armoury they can spare, such as spears, lances, swords and shields.
- Meanwhile, back in Madinah, Abdullah Jaffer, the husband of Lady Zainab and brother-in-law

and cousin of Imam Husein (as) (see Chart 1 on the inside back cover), takes two actions when he comes to know that Imam Husein (as) has left Makkah for Kufa.

- The first action is to request Amr Saeed, the Governor of Madinah and Makkah, to write a letter to Imam Husein (as) to guarantee him his safety if he were to remain in Makkah or Madinah.
- Amr Saeed writes this guarantee of safety and Abdullah tells him that it will carry more weight if it is delivered in person by the governor's brother, Yahya; Amr Saeed agrees to this also.
- The second action is to take his two children, Aun and Muhammad, with him to go and meet Imam Husein (as) (some reports say that these two children were with Imam Husein (as) when he left Madinah for Makkah).
- Abdullah Jaffer, his two children Aun and Muhammad, and Yahya Saeed cross paths with Imam Husein's (as) group at Tanim.
- Abdullah advises Imam Husein (as) not to go to Kufa for out of fear for safety, and tells him that his safety is guaranteed in Makkah and Madinah, as confirmed by the letter from the

governor delivered in person by the governor's brother.

- When he fails to persuade him, he tells him not to take the women and children with him; Imam Husein (as) tells him that he is taking them for a purpose (as explained in Section 5.5).

- Imam Husein (as) then tells Abdullah about a dream he had when the Prophet tells Imam Husein (as) to carry on with his mission; hence he is proceeding to Kufa despite the safety concerns raised by his family.

- Abdullah returns to Madinah because of his illness and leaves his two children to accompany Imam Husein (as).

Saffah

- The next stop is Saffah, a small village just outside of Makkah.

- Imam Husein (as) meets Farazdaq, the famous poet, who is from Iraq and is on his way to Makkah for the Hajj; he asks him about the mood of the people of Kufa.

- Farazdaq gives him the famous answer: "Their hearts are with you, but their swords are with the Umayyas".

- He also comes across some traders coming from Kufa; they tell him that his supporters in Kufa are waiting for him.

- Note that because of the time lag, this is now out-of-date news, as the situation has changed since these traders left Kufa.

7.3 Dhat-al-Irq, Batn-al-Rummah and Zarud

Dhat-al-Irq

- The next stop is Dhat-al-Irq.

- No particular historical event takes place at this location.

Batn-al-Rummah

- The next stop is Batn-al-Rummah.

- At this stopping point, Imam Husein (as) writes a letter to the people of Kufa.

- He writes that he has received the letter from Muslim Aqil saying there is a big support for him in Kufa, and that he is on his way; he has not yet received the news of the change in circumstances in Kufa.

- He gives it to Qays Mushir to take it to Kufa (he is the same messenger who brought the letters from Kufa, and from Muslim Aqil in Madiq).

- Some reports say that it is given to Abdullah Yaqtar, and not Qays Mushir; other reports say that Imam Husein (as) writes two letters and gives to Qays Mushir and Abdullah Yaqtar, at two different places along the journey.

Zarud

- The next stop is Zarud.
- As the Hajj period is now over, people are returning to their homes from Makkah; one such group is of Zuhayr Qayn going back to Kufa.
- Zuhayr Qayn was a supporter of the Leader Othman and not of the Prophet's Household; he has no intention to be involved with Imam Husein (as) and avoids any contacts with him; so, he and his group would stop either behind or ahead of the place where Imam Husein (as) has stopped.
- However, somehow they cross paths at Zarud.
- Imam Husein (as) sends a personal invitation to Zuhayr to come to his tent and meet him; Zuhayr, out of respect for Imam Husein (as), goes to meet him.

- Imam Husein (as) explains to him the reasons for his going to Kufa and why he is not recognising the government of Yazeed.

- Zuhayr becomes convinced of Imam Husein's (as) mission and comes back to his family to tell them that he has now decided to join the group of Imam Husein (as).

- A trader returning to Yemen from Kufa, sees Imam Husein's (as) group from a distance and he makes a deliberate detour to avoid any contact with them.

- Meanwhile, two people who have finished performing their Hajj are trying and want to join Imam Husein (as) are trying to catch up with him.

- They notice the Yemeni trader's odd conduct; for it is the ways of the desert travel that people will at the least exchange greetings on their way.

- They follow him to find out what the reason is.

- The trader tells them that Muslim Aqil and Hani Urwa were killed when he was in Kufa; he did not have the heart to tell this to Imam Husein (as) and so he avoided any contact.

7.4 Thalabiyyah and Zubalah

Thalabiyyah

- The next stop is Thalabiyyah.

- The two people who followed the Yemeni trader catch up with Imam Husein (as) and his group at Thalabiyyah.

- They tell Imam Husein (as) that they would like to inform him in private some bad news they have received from Kufa; Imam Husein (as) tells them he has no secrets from his group; so they tell of the martyrdom of Muslim Aqil and Hani Urwa.

- Imam Husein (as) then asks the family of Aqil (Muslim's brothers and sons) if they want to continue with the journey and they reply yes.

- Some reports say that, at this moment Imam Husein (as) offers a particular condolence to Hamida, a daughter of Muslim Aqil, and tells her that he will take care of her and treat like his daughter.

Zubalah

- The next stop is Zubalah.

- At this sopping point, Imam Husein (as) receives the news that one of his messengers, Abdullah Yaqtar, has also been martyred in Kufa.

- Abdullah Yaqtar was stopped by the security forces at Qadisiyyah, a town on the southern boundary of Kufa.

- He was found carrying the letter of Imam Husein (as) to the people of Kufa informing them that he is on his way.

- He was taken to Ubaydullah who told him that his punishment was death, unless he publicly spoke bad about Imam Husein (as) and his family.

- He was given the pulpit in the central mosque, but he refused to speak bad about Imam Husein (as) and the Prophet's Household to save his own life; he actually praised them.

- This infuriated Ubaydullah and he ordered that Abdullah Yaqtar should be thrown from the roof of the governor's palace; he died instantly.

- Imam Husein (as) also receives the message of Muslim Aqil telling him not to go to Kufa; this was the message that Muhammad Ashath dispatched upon the request of Muslim Aqil (see Section 6.7).

- Imam Husein (as) talks to his whole group covering three points.

- First, he tells them about the martyrdom of Abdullah Yaqtar.
- Second, he tells them of the message he has received from Muslim Aqil, asking him not to go to Kufa for the situation has changed there.
- Third, he tells them that what befell Muslim Aqil, Hani Urwa and Abdullah Yaqtar is what is awaiting them when they go to Kufa; so they should not entertain any hope of benefitting from the spoils of any battle, or gaining high office or power.
- He therefore tells them that should anyone want to leave him, now is the time do so, and they have his full blessings.
- The inference is that about thirty people (from about a hundred people who joined from Makkah) leave him; the inferred estimate is from the number of martyrs in Karbala and those who join him on the way and at Karbala.
- This different style of Imam Husein (as) is very much against all the commonly accepted norms of a leader; a leader would rally his group around him and not talk them into leaving him.
- However, Imam Husein (as) tells them of the situation exactly as it is, without glossing over or putting a different spin on the situation, for

he wants only the most dedicated and loyal people for his mission; he wants quality and not just quantity, for this is a battle of conscience versus might and not might versus might.

- He wants people who are ready to sacrifice their lives for the sake of safeguarding the Islamic ways.

7.5 Batn-al-Aqaba, Sharaf and Dhu Husum

Batn-al-Aqaba

- The next stop is Batn-al-Aqaba.
- Here, Imam Husein (as) gets the news that Ubaydullah's security forces are patrolling the southern boundary, thereby blocking any entry into Kufa from the south.
- If he were to continue on this route, he knows it will result in his arrest and killing, and his mission will end before it has even started.
- So he makes a detour and tries to enter Kufa through the western boundary; this will be a more difficult route as it passes through a very hilly ground.

Sharaf

- The next stop is Sharaf.
- This is an oasis and a major stopping point.
- Here, the supplies of food and water are stocked up.
- The new moon is sighted and the Islamic new year has set in; it is the eve of 1 Muharram 61 AH (30 September 680 AD).
- Imam Husein (as) and his group journey through the hilly region to arrive at the next stop point the following day.

Dhu Husum

- The next stop is Dhu Husum.
- It is the first day of the new month, 1 Muharram 61 AH (1 October 680 AD).
- Meanwhile, back in Kufa, Ubaydullah gets the report that Imam Husein (as) and his group are trying to enter Kufa from the western side.
- So he sends an army unit of about one thousand soldiers under the command of the army officer, Hurr ar-Riyahi.
- He instructs Hurr to arrest Imam Husein (as) and his group and to bring them as prisoners to Kufa.

- Imam Husein (as) and his group, and Hurr and his soldiers meet at Dhu Husum.

- Hurr and his soldiers have travelled through the mountainous and desert area from the western side of Kufa; by the time they reach Dhu Husum, they are thirsty and their water supply has run out.

- Imam Husein (as) instructs his group to supply water from their stock to the thirsty soldiers and animals (note the display of humanity by Imam Husein (as) in supplying water even to people who have come to arrest him - and contrast this with how he will be treated by Yazeed's forces later on).

- When the time for afternoon prayers come, Imam Husein (as) tells Hurr that he will be leading the prayers for his group and Hurr may wish to lead the prayers for his own group.

- Hurr replies that he and his group will also pray behind Imam Husein (as); note that Hurr has respect for Imam Husein (as) for he prays behind the person he has come to arrest, showing that he recognises the nobility and excellence of Imam Husein (as).

- As Imam Husein (as) and his group resume their journey to Kufa, they are blocked by Hurr and his soldiers.

- Hurr tells Imam Husein (as) that they can only go to Kufa as prisoners but not as free men; for that is the order of Ubaydullah Ziyad, the governor of Kufa.

- Imam Husein (as) tells Hurr that he is heading towards Kufa because of the invitations from the people of Kufa; Hurr says that he is not aware of them, so Imam Husein (as) shows him the letters written by the people of Kufa.

- There is now a standoff; Imam Husein (as) refuses to submit himself as a prisoner to Hurr; Hurr is not allowing him to go back to Madinah for his order is to bring Imam Husein (as) as a prisoner to Kufa.

- Hurr is now at a loss as to what action he should take; because of the respect that he has for Imam Husein(as), he does not wish to use force to take him to Kufa.

- So Hurr suggests a compromise; Imam Husein (as) will not take the south route leading to Madinah, nor will he take the east route leading to Kufa; he can take the north route and meanwhile, Hurr will inform Ubaydullah of the standoff and await his further orders.

- Imam Husein (as) agrees; so he and his group head north, with Hurr and his soldiers following behind.

7.6 Al-Baidah, Udhayb-al-Hijanat and Qasr-bani-Muqatil

Al-Baidah

- The next stop is Al-Baidah.
- Here, Imam Husein (as) addresses the soldiers of Hurr and highlights to them three main points.
- First, he reminds them of his lineage that he is the grand-son of the Prophet.
- Second, he tells them he is going to Kufa because of the many invitations from the people of Kufa themselves.
- Third, he explains to them why he is not pledging his allegiance to Yazeed for he:
    - is an unjust ruler
    - makes lawful what Allah has made unlawful
    - violates the rules of the Quran
    - challenges the ways and customs of the Prophet
    - openly indulges in sins of the worst kinds
- Pledging allegiance to such a ruler means the destruction of Islam, and he will not be a party to it.

Udhayb-al-Hijanat

- The next stop is Udhayb-al-Hijanat.

- Here, Imam Husein (as) gets the latest news of the situation in Kufa from a group of four people who have managed to bypass the security forces at the border:

    - Ubaydullah has imposed a state of emergency rule
    - he has bribed the tribal chiefs to turn against Imam Husein (as)
    - all borders are sealed
    - no public gatherings are allowed
    - security forces are on full alert
    - all able bodied men are conscripted into the army
    - the iron mongers are working flat out to make the armoury
    - units of soldiers are being prepared for a battle with Imam Husein (as) and his group

- Imam Husein (as) is also informed of the martyrdom of his second messenger, Qays Mushir; his capture and death are similar to Abdullah Yaqtar, the first messenger.

- The group of four people join Imam Husein (as) as his supporters.

Qasr-bani-Muqatil

- The next stop is Qasr-bani-Muqatil.
- This is a brief resting point.

7.7 Nainawa and Karbala

Nainawa

- The next stop is Nainawa.
- Nainawa is a hamlet, a small populated village, near the other hamlets of Ghadariyyah and Shafayyah.
- Here, Hurr receives his new orders from Ubaydullah Ziyad, the governor of Kufa.
- Ubaydullah admonishes Hurr for his accommodating attitude towards Imam Husein (as); he reminds him that his order was to bring in Imam Husein (as) as a prisoner and not to allow him any other choice.
- The order is composed of five instructions.
- First, upon receiving these instructions, Hurr must stop immediately from going any further.
- Second, he should position Imam Husein (as) and his group at an open area, well away from any vegetation land (for food supply) and

water supply; note that the plan of Ubaydullah to restrict the supply of food and water to Imam Husein (as) and his group is there from the start.

- Third, he should not take any further action until the arrival of a new commander who is being sent to replace him.

- Fourth, no one from Imam Husein's (as) group must be allowed to leave.

- Fifth, on his return to Kufa, the messenger has to confirm that these orders have been carried out.

- Hurr, under the supervision of the messenger, stops Imam Husein (as) and his group at an open area, away from the water supply, called Karbala, a very short distance from the village of Nainawa.

- Zohayr Qayn suggests to Imam Husein (as) that they can overpower Hurr and his soldiers and do not have to follow his instructions; he refuses to do so for he does not want to be the one to start the fight.

Karbala

- Karbala is a barren desert plain, near the village of Nainawa.

- River Euphrates is a very long river running through the three countries of Turkey, Syria and Iraq; one of its braches called Alqama, runs through the land of Karbala.

- Hurr positions Imam Husein (as) and his group well away from the bank of Alqama; he posts his guards along the bank so as to restrict the water supply to Imam Husein (as) and his group.

- Imam Husein (as) asks the local people for the name of this place; they tell him it is sometimes called Karbala; Imam Husein (as) then says that this is the place where his destiny will be realised.

- The word Karbala is composed of two words - Karb means grief or sorrow and Bala means afflictions; so the word Karbala means it is a land of grief and afflictions (as it will turn out to be for Imam Husein (as) and his group).

- It took about three weeks, since leaving Makkah on 8 Zillhajj 60 AH (9 September 680 AD), to cover a distance of about eight hundred miles from Makkah to Karbala with some stops in-between.

- The day is now Thursday, 2 Muharram 61 AH (2 October 680 AD).

8 At Karbala

In this chapter, we will describe what happens in Karbala during the next eight days since the arrival of Imam Husein (as) and his group and the incoming forces of Yazeed.

8.1 Buying the land

- A day after his arrival, on 3 Muharram 61 AH (3 October 680 AD), Imam Husein (as) calls the people of Karbala and the neighbouring villages of Nainawa, Ghadariyyah and Shafayyah.
- He offers to pay sixty thousand dinars for a freehold ownership of a piece of land of Karbala - belonging to the tribe of Banu Asad; this is an extremely generous price at the time.
- He imposes three conditions for the purchase of the land.
- First, he explained to the people of Banu Asad that soon he and his group would be killed and their bodies would be left unburied; he asked them to bury them after the army of Yazeed has left.

- Second, the land should remain as a cemetery and not cultivate the land around the gravesites.

- Third, they should host and be hospitable to pilgrims who will come to pay homage at their graves.

- The people of Banu Asad agree to this; Imam Husein (as) pays for the land; he then immediately gives it back to them as a gift.

- Until today, the conditions of Imam Husein (as) are being honoured by the local population of Karbala.

8.2 Appointment of Umar Saad

- Yazeed in Damascus is the Commander-in-Chief of the Muslim army; he has ordered Ubaydullah in Kufa to get the allegiance of Imam Husein (as) by any means.

- Imam Husein (as) in Karbala is surrounded by about one thousand soldiers under the command of Hurr.

- Meanwhile, Ubaydullah's first priority in Kufa is to very quickly mobilise an army unit and appoint a commander to take over from Hurr (for reasons explained in Section 7.7).

- There is a unit of about four thousand soldiers led by Umar Saad, stationed just outside Kufa, all prepared and ready for action.

- This unit is ready to head for Iran to recapture the province of Dastab (between present-day Tehran and Hamadan) which rebelled against the Syrian rule; Umar Saad is the commander of this unit; he is given a letter of appointment to be the governor of Rayy (a province of present-day Tehran), which will be his base.

- Ubaydullah orders him to go to Karbala first, take charge of the forces and obtain the allegiance of Imam Husein (as); he can then go to Iran.

- Umar Saad says he is not prepared to confront the grand-son of the Prophet; Ubaydullah then gives him an ultimatum - either go to Karbala or he will replace him for the Iranian campaign and thereby lose the governorship of Rayy.

- Umar Saad asks for a day to think over the matter; he consults his family and friends; they all advise him that he should not even think of going to Karbala to confront Imam Husein (as), the grand-son of the Prophet.

- The next day, Umar Saad tells Ubaydullah that he does not wish to go to Karbala, but gives him the names of other army officers who are willing to do so; Ubaydullah tells him that he has not asked for his advise, and as he does not want to go to Karbala, then he loses the governorship of Rayy.

- When Umar Saad realises that he will lose the governorship office, he agrees to go to Karbala first.

- Umar Saad with a unit of about four thousand soldiers heads for Karbala and arrives there on 3 Muharram 61 AH (3 October 680 AD).

8.3 Numbers on both sides

- There are about one thousand soldiers with Hurr when they stop at Karbala, on 2 Muharram 61 AH (2 October 680 AD).

- The next day, 3 Muharram, another unit of about four thousand soldiers arrive under Umar Saad who is to be the General of Yazeed's army in Karbala.

- For the next six days, from 4 Muharram to 9 Muharram, more and more soldiers from Kufa arrive in Karbala; army officers lead the units of cavalry, foot soldiers, archers and lancers.

- In Kufa, the ironmongers are working all hours to supply the armoury - hooves for the horses, spears, lances, swords, arrows and shields.

- It is about forty fives miles between Karbala and Kufa and a journey by horse takes about half a day.
- There are varying estimates (from about twenty thousand to one hundred and twenty thousand) in the literature about the total number of soldiers in Karbala on the side of Yazeed; however, the consensus is that there are about thirty thousand soldiers.
- All the soldiers are from Kufa; there are two reasons for this.
- First, Kufa was founded as a garrison town predominantly populated by soldiers; many of them still live there.
- Second, as Karbala is very near to Kufa, it makes sense to deploy local soldiers rather than dispatching them from Damascus or other cities.
- There are also varying estimates (from about seventy to one hundred and fifty) in the literature about the total number of males who died with Imam Husein (as).
- The consensus from the literature is that about one hundred and ten (other reports indicate one hundred and twenty) males, men

and children, died with Imam Husein (as); their names are also available (see Section 9.9).

- A figure of seventy two martyrs is usually quoted; the explanation is that only seventy two severed heads (from a total of about one hundred and ten martyrs) were brought to Kufa by Umar Saad's army; his soldiers refused to sever the heads of the rest of the martyrs as they had family or tribal relations with them.
- There were about forty women and children who survived the Karbala massacre.

8.4 Reasons for imbalance in numbers

Yazeed's side

- A question that comes to mind is this: how can a known tyrant and evil person like Yazeed assemble such a huge army against the grandson of the Prophet?
- There are about thirty thousand soldiers of Yazeed compared to about one hundred men with Imam Husein (as); this gives a ratio of three hundred to one; this is a huge imbalance between the two sides as far as manpower is concerned.
- This imbalance is explained by three factors.

- First, most of the army is composed of conscripts, that is, people are forced to take part because Ubaydullah has issued a decree that all able bodied men must enlist in the army; anyone evading this call faces punishment.

- Second, they are promised a government cash allowance on their return; so they are motivated to serve in the army.

- Third, Kufa has many reserves since the population is composed of professional soldiers who served in previous campaigns.

Imam Husein's (as) side

- There are five reasons to explain the small number on Imam Husein's (as) side.

- First, the core support for the Prophet's Household is from the people of Kufa; however since 41 AH (661 AD) when Muawiya was the political leader of the Muslims, they have been systematically sidelined and subjugated; this intensified over the years and especially in 60 AH (680 AD) when Ubaydullah came to Kufa (as we saw in Section 6.5) and imprisoned many of them.

- Second, Ubaydullah imposes a news blackout and misinformation in Kufa - this is a classic military strategy used to gain advantage over the enemy; so Imam Husein's (as) supporters, who are not in prison, are kept in the dark of his whereabouts and the danger he is in.

- Third, there are roadblocks around Kufa and Karbala to stop the supporters of Imam Husein (as) to get to him.

- Fourth, because of the change of destination from Kufa to Karbala, some of the supporters of Imam Husein (as) are unable to reach him in time.

- Fifth, Imam Husein (as) does not force people to join him or to remain with him; he encourages them to leave him for his mission is one of sacrifice and not of any gain.

8.5 Intermediary meeting between Imam Husein (as) and Umar Saad

- Umar Saad wants to explore a way out of his commitment to confront Imam Husein (as).

- On the day of his arrival in Karbala, 3 Muharram 61 AH (3 October 680 AD), he sends one of his men, Qurra Hanzali, to find out from Imam Husein (as) what has brought him to Karbala and what is his plan of action now.

- Imam Husein (as) tells him that he did not want to come to Karbala, but was to go to Kufa at the invitation of many people there; since the situation has changed there, he is ready to go back to his hometown in Madinah.

- It should be noted that Imam Husein (as) is offering a peaceful and amicable solution without having to compromise his principled stand not to pledge allegiance to Yazeed; he is trying to avoid a confrontation if at all possible.

- Umar Saad is surprised at this very accommodating position of Imam Husein (as), for the impression given to him by Ubaydullah is that Imam Husein (as) is a rebel and is out to cause problems, at any cost, for Yazeed and his government.

- Umar Saad senses a chance to diffuse the crisis; he writes to his commander Ubaydullah in Kufa that there is no need to force a confrontation with Imam Husein (as) for he is willing to go back to Madinah.

- Ubaydullah replies that since Imam Husein (as) has been cornered, he is trying to find a way out; he commands Umar Saad to "get the allegiance from Imam Husein (as) and then we will decide what to do with him".

- This order shows very clearly that even if Imam Husein (as) were to pledge allegiance to Yazeed, his freedom and safety are not guaranteed.

- When Umar Saad receives this order, he realises that the prospect of a battle with Imam Husein (as) is now real and unavoidable.

8.6 Direct meeting between Imam Husein (as) and Umar Saad

- Imam Husein (as) sends Amr Qarazah to Umar Saad to ask for a one-to-one meeting in private.

- This is unheard of in a battle zone, where two leaders on the opposite side engage in a one-to-one private meeting; either it takes place in the open with others present, or it is the deputies of the leaders who meet.

- Imam Husein (as) is asking for this private meeting for two reasons.

- First, he wants to explore all avenues for peace; he wants to ensure that history records he is not intent on a battle, but is willing to find a peaceful solution (without compromising his principled opposition to Yazeed).

- Second, he wants to avoid talking to intermediaries in case there is any manipulation, distortion or exaggeration of his position.

- This meeting takes place at night on the eve of 8 Muharram 61 AH (7 October 680 AD); this date is inferred by the timing of the subsequent events.

- Imam Husein (as) and Umar Saad each come with about twenty of their men; they meet about halfway between the two camp sites.

- Imam Husein (as) asks his men to leave and so does Umar Saad; the two men now meet in private.

- Imam Husein (as) repeats what he had told Qurra Hanzali on 3 Muharram; he emphasises that he is ready to go back to Madinah and now offers even to leave Arabia.

- Umar Saad now hears first-hand of Imam Husein's (as) very accommodating position; he writes to Ubaydullah that a solution has been found to avoid any battle with Imam Husein (as) for he has even agreed to leave Arabia.

- Meanwhile, Ubaydullah sends an order to Umar Saad which reaches him on 7 Muharram 61 AH (7 October 680 AD); the order is to cut off completely any water supply to Imam Husein's (as) side; as it is, the water supply was very restricted from the day of their arrival in Karbala.

- Even more armed soldiers are now positioned along the river bank to stop any attempts by the men of Imam Husein (as) to get any water.

8.7 Arrival of Shimr Ziljawshan

- The letter of Umar Saad reaches Ubaydullah, by inference of events, on 8 Muharram 61 AH (8 October 680 AD) in the presence of an army officer by the name of Shimr Ziljawshan.

- Ubaydullah appears to be impressed by the efforts of Umar Saad in trying to avoid a confrontation with Imam Husein (as), but Shimr stiffens his resolve.

- Ubaydullah replies to Umar Saad that he was not sent as a negotiator or an intercessor; the order is to get Imam Husein's (as) allegiance, bring him as a prisoner to Kufa and then a decision will be made about his fate.

- He orders that if no allegiance is forthcoming from Imam Husein (as), then he should be engaged in a battle, killed, mutilated and his body trampled by horses.

- Furthermore, Umar Saad is to carry out this order immediately or hand over the command of the army to Shimr Ziljawshan.

- Abdullah Abi Muhil, another army officer, is present when this order is made.

- Ummul Baneen, the wife of Imam Ali (as) is the aunt of Abdullah Abi Muhil; her four children - Abbas, Jaffer, Othman and Abdullah - are brothers of Imam Husein (as) and they are with him in Karbala (see Chart 1 on the inside back cover); he asks Ubaydullah for a letter to guarantee the safety for his four cousins; this is given.

- Shimr, with a unit of about four thousand soldiers, arrives in Karbala on Thursday, 9 Muharram 61 AH (9 October 680 AD) late in the afternoon.

- He goes to Umar Saad immediately and presents him with the order; he challenges him to carry it out or to give up his command and hand it over to Shimr; Umar Saad tells him that he will carry out the orders immediately.

- Shimr then goes to see the sons of Ummul Baneen and guarantees their safety if they leave Imam Husein (as); they are outraged and curse Shimr for not offering such a guarantee of safety to the grand-son of the Prophet.

- Umar Saad, with a contingent of his army officers and soldiers, come over to the camp of Imam Husein (as).

- Imam Husein (as) sends his brother Abbas (see Chart 1 on the inside back cover) - the flag bearer of Imam Husein's (as) group - with about twenty other supporters, to enquire about their aggressive approach so late in the day.

- Umar Saad informs Abbas of the ultimatum from Ubaydullah: Imam Husein (as) has got to pledge his allegiance to Yazeed now, either peacefully or extracted forcefully in a battle.

- When informed of this, Imam Husein (as) sends Abbas to request a postponement for the night and for the matter to be decided the following morning.

- Umar Saad consults with his officers and the request is granted.

8.8 The last night

- Dusk has now set in; it is Thursday, eve of 10 Muharram 61 AH (9 October 680 AD).
- Imam Husein (as) is requesting a postponement for four reasons.
- There is no question of him asking the postponement in order to consider if he is going to pledge allegiance to Yazeed; this is completely out of the question.
- He never will and never would, in any circumstances, pledge allegiance to Yazeed.

First reason for postponement

- Imam Husein (as) wants both sides to reflect in the quiet of the night.
- The soldiers on the opposite side are now all psyched up in preparation for the battle; now that the actual moment is here, he wants them to reflect on what they are planning to do, and the consequences of their actions.
- He is giving them a chance to reconsider their plan, so they cannot give the excuse they had no time to reflect because they had been overwhelmed with a momentum of the ensuing battle.

- The companions of Imam Husein (as) are also given the chance to decide whether they want to stay with him or leave him.

- This night of reflection has the desired effect on both sides; both sides now make their decision in a calm and unhurried way and choose their destiny.

Second reason for postponement

- Imam Husein (as) wants to talk to his group; there are about ninety male adults with him, and about twenty males (adults, youths and children) from his own family.

- He gathers them all, and talks to them; his talk is simple, factual and minimal for he wants them to make a decision rationally; he covers five points.

- First, he draws their attention to the sounds from Yazeed's camp; it is the sound of war drums beating and armoury being sharpened; he tells them that they are after him and him alone, but they will not spare anyone who gets in their way; so they should leave and they will get a safe passage back to their homes, for the opposite side will be glad to see people abandoning him.

- Second, he acknowledges that he could not wish for any better relatives or supporters, for they are the best; he gives them his full blessings and permission to leave him and he promises them that he will hold no grudges against them, either in this world or in the Hereafter.

- Third, he completely absolves them of any social or moral obligation they have towards him as their relative, friend or Imam.

- Fourth, he prays to Allah to grant them great rewards for their support so far.

- Fifth, he tells them that should anyone be hesitating to leave him because they feel ashamed, he is going to get all the lamps turned off, so they can leave in the darkness unnoticed; after a while he asks for the lamps to be lit and sees that not even one person has left him.

- Note that this approach is very different from the conventional; here, a leader is asking his supporters to leave freely and unhindered, whereas normally a leader would be energising his troops to stick together and fight the enemy; he wants people with him who are truly and deeply committed to his mission.

- Three persons now answer Imam Husein (as); each one of them echoes the sentiments of the three groups of people they represent.

- Abbas, the brother of Imam Husein (as) and the spokesman of his family speaks first.

- He says the family gives a solemn promise that they will never leave Imam Husein (as) out of their sight, for it will never be that they are alive and see him killed first.

- Muslim Awsaja, an elder from Kufa and the spokesman of the friends of the Prophet's family speaks next.

- He says they will never leave Imam Husein (as) to face the enemy alone; he asks what answer they would give to Allah on the Day of Judgement when asked why they did not help and defend Imam Husein (as).

- He says they are prepared to endure all sufferings on the battlefield, and they will fight to their death with all their strength and weapons at their disposal, even if they are just left with stones.

- Next to speak is Zuhayr Qayn, the spokesman of the group of people who joined Imam Husein (as) en-route from Makkah and those who joined him from Kufa.

- He says that if it is possible to die once, come alive and die again, then they are prepared to die a thousand such deaths to save Imam Husein (as) and his family from the enemies.

Third reason for postponement

- Imam Husein (as) puts up a defence around his tents for the safety of the women and children for he anticipates an attack from the rear.

- He wants all the tents pitched closer together and inter-connected by tying them to one another.

- Finally, he gets a trench dug behind the tents filled up with firewood; when set alight this will slow down any surprise attacks.

Fourth reason for postponement

- When all the defences are in place, Imam Husein (as) gathers his group.

- He tells them that this is their last night in this world.

- They spend the night worshipping Allah, engaged in supplications and recitation of the Quran.

- Literature records that the sounds of the prayers like the humming of the bees.

- By contrast the army of Yazeed spend the night in laughter, merry making, and sharpening their armoury.

9 Ashura Day

Friday, 10 Muharram 61 AH

Friday, 10 October 680 AD

The tenth day of the month has arrived; in Arabic language, the tenth is termed Ashura; hence this day is known as Ashura; Ashura day specifically refers to the tenth of Muharram, the day that marks the events that occurred in Karbala.

In this chapter, we will follow the events as they unfold on this day, on the plains of Karbala, from early dawn to late night. We will look at the way the battle is conducted on both sides, and in particular the losses on Imam Husein's (as) side.

9.1 Dawn

- The dawn of the day of Ashura is here; both sides are preparing for the dawn (Fajr) prayers.
- Imam Husein (as) asks his second son, Ali Akbar (see Chart 1 on the inside back cover of the book), to call the Adhan (the prayer call); he chooses him for a particular reason.
- Ali Akbar is the image of the Prophet in every respect; his face resembles that of the

Prophet; his walking style imitates that of the Prophet; his manners reflect that of the Prophet; even his voice resonates that of the Prophet.

- There are people in Yazeed's army who were with the Prophet; this action is meant to remind them that they are fighting the grandson of their Prophet.
- Imam Husein (as) leads the prayers for his group; this will be his last full congregational prayer.
- Umar Saad leads the prayers for his own group.

9.2 Early morning - Imam Husein (as) speaks

- After prayers, both sides now position their groups to face each other.
- Imam Husein (as) mounts a camel and faces the soldiers of Yazeed; a camel symbolises a conciliatory and friendly gesture.
- Some reports say he mounts a horse, which is regarded as an aggressive and hostile gesture.
- He addresses them at the top of his voice and covers five points.

First point - know the facts

- He draws their attention to the need to know some facts before engaging in a battle.

- He tells them that after he has given them the facts, they should then deal with him justly and they would be happier for it.

- He says to them that should they decide not to be just with him, then they should agree upon their course of action amongst themselves, and they should not delay their actions any further.

Second point - identity

- It is possible that the lineage and the personality of Imam Husein (as) is not known to all the soldiers who have gathered in Karbala.

- He has been portrayed by the authorities in Damascus and Kufa as a common rebel out to cause problems for the government of Yazeed; they are not told why Imam Husein (as) is not ready to pledge his allegiance to Yazeed.

- All these soldiers are Muslims and so they have definitely heard of the Prophet and his family.

- It is important that Imam Husein (as) makes his identity known, so they cannot claim later on they were not aware of his connection to the Prophet's Household.

- He identifies himself in relation to the Prophet by these questions:
    - Am I not the grand-son of your Prophet?
    - Am I not the son of the daughter of your Prophet?
    - Am I not the son of the executor of the will of the Prophet (meaning Imam Ali (as))?
    - Is not Hamza, the Lord of the Martyrs, my uncle?
    - Is not Jaffer, who is flying with two wings in Paradise, my uncle?
    - Did not the Prophet say that Hasan and Husein are the leaders of the youths of Paradise? I am that Husein.

- He then says he has never ever lied before and is not lying now.

- If they still doubt him, they should ask some of their officers who know of his status and have even heard the Prophet talk about his two grand-sons, Hasan and Husein.

- He asks them, now that they know his connection to the Prophet's Household, are they still prepared to kill him?

Third point - motive

- Imam Husein (as) now wants to identify their motive why they are intent on killing him.

- He asks them if they are seeking revenge for any reason:

  - Have I killed any of your relations?
  - Have I stolen any of your property?
  - Have I inflicted any injury to you?

Fourth point - reason for coming

- He then goes on to tell them he is in Karbala under duress and by force.

- His intention was to go to Kufa at the written invitations of many people of Kufa.

- He even points out to some army officers by name who have written these invitations.

Fifth point - possible solution

- He now offers them a way out; he says he is ready to go back to any place where his security is guaranteed.

- Note that in making this offer, he is not changing his principled stand of refusing to pledge allegiance to Yazeed.

- Qays Ashath, an army officer, asks Imam Husein (as) why he does not submit to the authority of Yazeed and no harm will come to him; Imam Husein (as) answers that he will never submit to anyone like a humiliated man, and neither will he run away like a slave.

9.3 Early morning - Zuhayr and Hurr speak

Zuhayr Qayn speaks

- After Imam Husein (as) has finished his talk, Zuhayr Qayn speaks to the soldiers of Yazeed.
- It just may be that the soldiers might listen to him, as he is a native of Kufa.
- He pleads with the soldiers not to kill Imam Husein (as).
- He contrasts for them the evils of Yazeed and Ubaydallah with the nobility of Imam Husein (as).
- He warns them of the divine punishment if they proceed to kill Imam Husein (as).
- He cautions them that the Prophet will not intercede for a community that sheds the blood of his family.
- The soldiers do not listen to him either.

Hurr ar-Riyahi speaks

- Hurr ar-Riyahi is the elite military officer of Yazeed's army who intercepted Imam Husein (as) at Dhu Husum and brought him to Karbala.

- Since his arrival in Karbala, he sees how Imam Husein (as), his family and his companions are being treated by the forces of Yazeed, for nine days.

- Furthermore, he feels he is responsible for the predicament they are in, for he brought them to Karbala.

- Since dawn he has been considering to change sides and after hearing Imam Husein (as), he decides to do so.

- He comes over to Imam Husein (as) and tells him that he never imagined it would end like this; he asks for repentance and Imam Husein (as) forgives him.

- He asks Imam Husein (as) for permission to speak to the soldiers, in the hope they would listen to him, as he was (until moments ago) from their side.

- He pleads with the soldiers and Umar Saad to accept the offer of Imam Husein (as) to go to a place where his safety is guaranteed, thereby avoiding any battle; Umar Saad says this is not an option.

- Hurr reminds the soldiers from Kufa that it was they who invited Imam Husein (as) and are now betraying him; it was they who promised to support him and are now ready to kill him.

- Eleven people from Yazeed's army change sides and join Imam Husein (as).

9.4 The battle begins - to late morning

- Imam Husein (as) has now tried everything in his power to avoid any bloodshed and come to a peaceful resolution.

- Both sides now line up their units; it is now clear that a battle has to be fought.

- Imam Husein (as) positions his group into three fronts to face the enemy.

- The right front of his group is headed by Habib Mazaher, his childhood friend, who managed to bypass the border patrols at Kufa and join him.

- The left front of his group is headed by Zuhayr Qayn, the man he befriended at Zarud en-route from Makkah.

- The central front of his group is headed by his brother, Abbas, the standard-bearer of Imam Husein (as).

- Imam Husein (as) lights the fire in the trench that was dug up the night before to slow down any assault from behind the battle line.

- The battle is fought in the traditional Arab way of warfare.

- A soldier on one side identifies himself by his tribal lineage and challenges a response to a single combat from the opposite side; the opposing fighter would step forward and also offer his tribal connections.

- There then follows a one-to-one fighting until one of the two persons is killed, and his place is taken by another fighter.

- Such duel challenges and fighting goes on till one side overpowers the other and come out as victors.

- The two sides are now positioned for the battle.

- Umar Saad declares to all his soldiers to witness that he starts the battle by arching an arrow to the bow and shoots towards the side of Imam Husein (as).

- Such one-to-one fighting goes on from early morning to about an hour before noon; in this period, eleven martyrs fall from the side of Imam Husein (as).

List and chronology of martyrs

- The full list and the order (chronology) in which the martyrs fall is given at the end of this chapter; historical records show a number of variations on this; the reader should not be fixated on the exact numbers and exact chronology, as this does not alter the nature of the gravity of the massacre in Karbala.

- The discipline is such that every person who goes to the battlefield first obtains permission from Imam Husein (as); only when this is granted does he then proceed to the battlefield.

- There is unanimity in the literature that the family members of Imam Husein (as) are martyred after all his companions have fallen; so, by inference, the companions of Imam Husein (as) are resolute that as long as they are alive, they do not allow any of Imam Husein's (as) family member to face the enemy.

- The first person to go to the battlefield is Abdullah Kalbi (also known as Wahab), but he comes back after some time; Hurr goes in second, but he also comes back after some time.

- The first martyr in Karbala is Muslim Awsaja.
- The only female martyred in Karbala is the wife of Abdullah Kalbi (Wahab); she runs to the battlefield, when her husband falls on the ground, to congratulate him on his sacrifice for Imam Husein (as); Shimr Ziljawshan, an army officer from the opposite side, gives the order for her to be killed.
- Imam Husein (as) makes sure that the body of each martyr is moved from the battlefield to a tent, which serves as a makeshift morgue; this is to ensure their bodies do not get trampled by the horse's hooves on the battlefield.
- There are two exceptions to this; Abbas, the brother of Imam Husein (as) is martyred by the river bank when trying to get water for Sukaina (the five year old daughter of Imam Husein (as)) and other children; he requests that his body is not taken back to the tent for he feels ashamed at not fulfilling the request of the children.
- The second exception is the body of Ali Asghar, the six month old baby of Imam Husein (as); he buries his body behind his tent in the hope that it will not be unearthed by the

enemy who he fears may want to behead all the martyrs; sadly, the enemy unearth his body and behead it.

9.5 The battle continues - to afternoon

- Umar Saad sees that in the one-to-one fighting so far, his side is loosing more men than Imam Husein's (as) side.
- He therefore changes the rules of engagement, against all the accepted warfare norms, he orders a general attack.
- A unit of about five hundred archers shoot arrows simultaneously at the side of Imam Husein's (as).
- In the general attack forty nine martyrs fall; this brings the total to sixty.
- None of Imam Husein's (as) family member is killed in this general attack; the inference is that the companions acted as human shields to protect Imam Husein (as) and his family members and they took the onslaught of the attack.
- The general attack and the sudden heavy loss on Imam Husein's (as) side gives an advantage to Umar Saad's side.

- Next, Shimr Ziljawshan, an army officer, with some soldiers rush to the back of the tents to attack from behind.

- However, their progress is slowed down by the fire in the trench surrounding the tents.

- Two martyrs fall in repelling the attack; this brings the total to sixty two martyrs.

Afternoon prayer time

- The time for afternoon (Zohar) prayer is approaching.

- Abu Thumama tells Imam Husein (as) that he would prefer to say his Zohar prayers first before going to the battlefield.

- Imam Husein (as) sends three of his companions to ask for a suspension of the battle so that the prayers can be said.

- This request is turned down despite the pleas by three eminent people of Kufa: Abu Thumama, Habib Mazaher and Hurr ar-Riyyahi; a battle follows and they are all martyred.

- This brings the total to sixty five martyrs.

- Imam Husein (as) leads a shortened prayer which is performed in times of danger and war.

- Two companions, Saeed Abdullah and Zuhayr Qayn stand as human shields in front of Imam Husein (as) while he leads the prayers; they die of wounds from the arrows being thrown at Imam Husein's (as) side.

- This brings the total to sixty seven martyrs.

Afternoon

- After prayers, there are twenty four companions left with Imam Husein (as).

- They are now more than determined to sacrifice their lives in defence of Imam Husein (as) and his family; the inference is that they do not allow any of his family members to go to the battlefield.

- They each go to the battlefield in turn.

- The rules of engagement are changed again by Umar Saad and his officers; after a while of one-to-one fighting, a group of soldiers would then ambush, surround and kill the one fighter from the side of Imam Husein (as).

- All the twenty four companions are martyred.

- By late afternoon, the total number of martyrs is ninety one.

- The full list and the chronology of the martyrs is at the end of this chapter; for each person, it shows where he is from (where known), and any other known details about him.

- It is significant to note that about two thirds of the companions come from the city of Kufa; this shows their dedication and loyalty to Imam Husein (as), for they manage to reach him despite the border patrols at Kufa and Karbala.

- The full breakdown of the number of companions is fifty nine from Kufa, nine from Basra, nine from Madinah, four from Makkah and ten whose home cities are unknown.

9.6 The family's turn to sacrifice

(Refer to Chart 8 on page 263)

- With all the companions of Imam Husein (as) now fallen, it is now the turn of his family members to go to the battle filed in defence of Islam and Imam Husein (as).

- They are all from the clan of Abu Talib.

- One by one, they come to ask for permission from Imam Husein (as) before they go to the battlefield.

- As they fall as martyrs, their bodies are brought back to a tent, which serves as a makeshift morgue (except for the bodies of Abbas and Ali Asghar, as discussed in Section 9.4).

- The first group to go to the battlefield is from the family of Aqil, the son of Abu Talib.

- The first two martyrs are the two children of Muslim Aqil – Abdullah and Muhammad (his first two young boys accompanied him to Kufa and are martyred there about one year later).

- The next three martyrs are the sons of Aqil – Jaffer, Abd Rahman and Abdullah.

- The last member from this group is Aqil's grand-son, Muhammad, the son of Saeed.

- This brings the total of martyrs from the family members to six.

- The next group of martyrs is from the family of Jaffer, the son of Abu Talib.

- They are the grand-sons of Jaffer, the sons of Abdullah and Lady Zainab - Muhammad, an eight year old, and Aun, a nine year old.

- This brings the total of martyrs from the family members to eight

- The next group of martyrs is from the family of Ali, the son of Abu Talib.

- The first two martyrs are the grand-sons of Imam Ali (as), the sons of Imam Hasan (as) - Qasim, a thirteen year old and Ahmed, a twelve year old.

- The next five martyrs are the sons of Imam Ali (as) - Muhammad (his mother is Laila), and Othman, Jaffer, Abdullah and Abbas (their mother is Ummul Baneen).

- The next two martyrs are the grand-sons of Imam Ali (as), the two sons of Imam Husein (as) - Ali Akbar, an eighteen year old, and Ali Asghar, a six month old baby (killed by an arrow when his father is pleading for some water to be given to him).

- The body of the six month old baby, Ali Asghar, is the only one that is buried on Ashura Day; Imam Husein (as) himself buries the baby behind his tent.

- This brings the total of martyrs from the family members to seventeen.

9.7 Martyrdom of Imam Husein (as)

- With all his companions and family members martyred, Imam Husein (as) is the only male adult left from his side, except for his twenty two year old first son, Ali Zainul Abedeen (see Chart 1 on the inside back cover of the book).

- He is too ill to participate in the battle, and the illness is intermittently causing him deep drowsiness; this is divine intervention for he becomes the fourth Imam after the martyrdom of his father.

- There is one eleven year old young boy, Abdullah, the son of Imam Hasan (as), who is still alive.

- Apart from these two, all the others are women and small girls and boys.

- Imam Husein (as) now comes to the tents of his family and says his final farewells to them.

- He then asks for a pair of old trousers which he tears up in places and wears under his normal clothes, fearing that should the enemies want to rob him of his clothes after his death, at least they would leave him covered with the torn trousers.

- He goes into the battlefield, engages in a fierce fight with the opposite side and inflicts significant losses and causalities; he also manages to cause panic and disarray in their formations.

- On seeing the bravery of Imam Husein (as) and the damage he is doing to his troops, Umar Saad orders a full assault on him; Imam Husein (as) is now surrounded by soldiers, and is hit by a volley of arrows from all sides; one arrow hits him on the forehead and he can no longer maintain his balance on his horse, and he falls on the ground.

- The next martyr is the grand-son of Imam Ali (as), the son of Imam Hassan (as) - Abdullah, an eleven year old; he dies of his injuries when he stretches his hands to shield Imam Husein (as) from a swinging sword aimed at him.

- For some considerable moments, none of the enemy soldiers dare to come forward and kill him; after a while, Shimr Ziljawshan shouts to the surrounding soldiers to kill him; some injure him with spears, some with swords and those with no armoury, use stones; Imam Husein (as) is now severely and multiply wounded and covered in his own blood.

- Sinan, one of the army officers stabs him with a spear, first through his throat, and then through his chest; Shimr Ziljawshan then kneels on the chest of Imam Husein (as), and grabs his beard, and then uses a dagger to behead him.

- The supreme, unique and ultimate sacrifice by Imam Husein (as) is now complete.

- Imam Husein (as) was born on 3 Shaban 4 AH (626 AD), and is martyred on 10 Muharram 61 AH (680 AD) at the age of fifty six years, going to fifty seven years.

- The head of Imam Husein (as) is mounted on a spear.

- Umar Saad orders that the head of Imam Husein (as) be immediately sent to Kufa to Ubaydallah; an army officer by the name of Khooli takes the severed head to Kufa.

9.8 The tyranny continues

- After the inhumane way in which Imam Husein (as) is murdered, Umar Saad's tyranny does not stop there.

- He orders ten horse riders to ride over the body of Imam Husein (as) and trample it with the horse's hooves.

- The tyranny continues; Imam Husein's (as) body is robbed of his turban, his sword, his sandals, and even all his clothes are stripped off his body, including the torn trousers that he put on.

- They leave his body naked and unburied on the sandy plains of Karbala.

- Such despicable treatment of a dead person is unheard of in Arabia; the soldiers of Yazeed behave in the most inhuman, outrageous and deplorable way.

- Umar Saad wants all the bodies of the companions and the family of Imam Husein (as) to be brought out from the tent (which serves as a makeshift morgue) to the open battlefield.

- He orders to behead all the bodies of the companions and the family of Imam Husein (as); some soldiers refuse to do so for some bodies as they are related by family or tribe.

- He also orders the search of the body of the six month old baby, Ali Asghar, and for his head to be severed also.

- The heads are then mounted on spears, and distributed amongst some army officers to take back to Kufa on the same day; they will be paraded through the streets of Kufa and later on in Damascus.

- Literature shows that there were seventy two heads plus the head of Imam Husein (as) in total.

- The night of the dispossessed is now beginning.

- The survivors are one male adult (Imam Ali Zainul Abedeen (as) - the eldest son of Imam Husein (as)), who is very ill, the ladies and the young children; some sources indicate that this is a group of about forty people.

- They are dispossessed of their fathers, husbands, brothers, uncles, nephews and the supporters of the Prophet's household

- The tyranny of Umar Sad continues.

- He orders that all their belongings should be looted; his soldiers enter their tents and steal any thing they can lay their hands on; they are dispossessed of their belongings.

- They steal any jewellery the ladies have on them; they are disposed of their jewellery.

- They even tear the veils off the ladies; they are dispossessed of their veils.

- They go further and rip off the clothes from the ladies and children; they are dispossessed of their clothing.

- The tyranny continues; Umar Saad orders that all the tents must be burnt; as each tent is set on fire, they run for shelter and safety from one tent to another, until they reach the last tent.
- When the last tent is also on fire, they now have no choice but to come out in the open sky, without their veils and their clothing ripped; they are dispossessed of their shelter.
- Imam Ali Zainul Abedeen, ill as he is, also leaves the last burning tent.
- The day of Ashura is over; the sun has set and the night is settling in.
- The survivors spend the night under the open sky, on the plains of the desert of Karbala; their family and friends are lying dead, many beheaded and their bodies unburied.
- This is the tragedy of Karbala.
- The Prophet's Household is dispossessed of all.
- Tonight is the night of the dispossessed.

9.9 List and chronology of martyrs

As discussed in Section 9.4, the actual number of martyrs on Ashura Day on the side of Imam Husein (as) is not exactly known, and literature has given various estimates; furthermore, the names and order (chronology) in which they are killed are also subject to the same historical variations.

The reader should not be fixated on the actual numbers, names and chronology. These variations do not alter the nature of the gravity and tyranny of the events on Ashura Day.

The list and chronology given below is a version compiled from the literature.

Morning

1 Muslim Awsaja al-Asadi — from Kufa
one of Muslim Aqil's deputy rallying support for Imam;
seen Prophet; expert horse-rider

2 Abdullah Umayr al-Kalbi (also known as Wahab); — from Kufa
companion of Imam Ali;
first on the battlefield but came back;
his wife was also killed (the only woman killed at Karbala)

3 Buryar Hudayr al-Hamdani — from Kufa
Quran teacher

4 Munhij Sahm — from Madinah
his mother (was at Karbala) was working in Imam's house

5 Umar Khalid — from Kufa
joined Imam at Udhayb-al-Hijanat

6 Saad — from Kufa
joined Imam at Udhayb-al-Hijanat

7	Mujammi Abdullah companion of Imam Ali; was at Battle of Siffin; joined Imam at Udhayb-al-Hijanat	from Kufa
8	Aidh Mujammi Abdullah companion of Imam Ali; was at Battle of Siffin; joined Imam at Udhayb-al-Hiijanat	from Kufa
9	Jabir al-Harith al-Salmani joined Imam at Udhayb-al-Hijanat	from Kufa
10	Jundub Hujr al-Kindi companion of Imam Ali; was at Battle of Siffin; joined Imam at Sharaf	from Kufa
11	Yazeed Ziyad al-Kindi expert archer; joined Imam at Sharaf	from Kufa

Late Morning: general attack

12	Al-Harith Banham house helper of Imam Ali, Imam Hasan, Imam Husein	from Madinah
13	Shabib al-Nashali was at Battles of Jamal, Siffin, Nahrawan	from Madinah
14	Qarib Abdullah his mother was a helper of Rubab (Imam's wife)	from Madinah
15	Nasr Nayzar in his youth, he kept company with Imam Ali, then with Imam Hasan, Imam Husein	from Madinah
16	Janada Kab al-Ansari	from Makkah
17	Abd Rahman Abd Rabb	from Makkah
18	Jabir Hajjaj al-Taymi	from Kufa
19	Jabla Ali al-Shaybani	from Kufa
20	Hubab Amir Kab al-Taymi	from Kufa
21	Zarghama Malik al-Taghlabi	from Kufa

22	Harith Imru Qays Abis Yazeed's army - changed sides	from Kufa
23	Juwayn Malik Qays al-Taymi Yazeed's army - changed sides	from Kufa
24	Halas Amr al-Azdi Yazeed's army - changed sides	from Kufa
25	Numan Amr al-Azdi Yazeed's army - changed sides	from Kufa
26	Zuhayr Salim Amr al-Azdi Yazeed's army - changed sides	from Kufa
27	Masud Hajjaj al- Taymi Yazeed's army - changed sides	from Kufa
28	Abd Rahman Masud Yazeed's army - changed sides	from Kufa
29	Abdullah Bishr al-Kathami Yazeed's army - changed sides	from Kufa
30	Amr Zabia Qays al-Taymi Yazeed's army - changed sides	from Kufa
31	Qasim Habib Abi Bishr al-Azdi Yazeed's army - changed sides	from Kufa
32	Abdullah Yazeed Nubayt joined Imam at Makkah	from Basra
33	Ubaydullah Yazeed Nubayt joined Imam at Makkah; (brother of Martyr 32)	from Basra
34	Adham Umayya joined Imam at Makkah	from Basra
35	Sayf Malik al-Abdi joined Imam at Makkah	from Basra
36	Amir Muslim Abdi al-Basri joined Imam at Makkah	from Basra

37	Salim joined Imam at Makkah	from Basra
38	Salim helper of Imam Hasan	from Makkah
39	Abd Muhajir al-Juhani	from Kufa
40	Uqba Salat al-Juhani	from Kufa
41	Mujammi Ziyad Amr al-Juhani	from Kufa
42	Qasit Zuhayr al-Harith companion of Imam Ali	from Kufa
43	Musqit Zuhayr al-Harith companion of Imam Ali	from Kufa
44	Kardus Zuhayr al-Harith companion of Imam Ali; (Martyrs 42, 43 and 44 are brothers)	from Kufa
45	Umayya Saad Zayd al-Tai was at Battle of Siffin	
46	Zahir Amr al-Kindi companion of Prophet; was at Khaybar; joined Imam at Makkah	from Kufa
47	Shabib Abdullah companion of Prophet; was at Battles of Jamal, Siffin, Nahrawan	from Kufa
48	Abd Rahman Abdullah Kadan	from Kufa
49	Ammar Abi Salama al-Dulani was at Battles of Jamal, Siffin, Nahrawan	
50	Ammar Hasan al-Tai	from Makkah
51	Kinana Atiq al-Taghlabi	from Kufa
52	Muslim Qasir al-Azdi was at Battle of Jamal; crippled	from Kufa

53	Naim Ajlan al-Ansari companion of Imam Ali	from Kufa
54	Habsha Qays al-Nahmi	from Kufa
55	Hajjaj Ziyad al-Taymi	from Basra
56	Habab Harith	
57	Hanzala Umar al-Shaybani	
58	Zuhayr Busr al-Khathami	
59	Imran Kab al-Ashjai	
60	Mani Ziyad	

Defending Imam's tents site

61	Bakr Hayy al-Taymi Yazeed's army, changed sides	from Kufa
62	Amr Janada Kab al-Khazraji ten years old (son of Martyr 17)	from Kufa

Asking for a suspension for noon prayers

63	Habib Mazaher companion of Imam Ali, Imam Hasan, Imam Husein; commander of Imam's unit	from Kufa
64	Hurr ar-Riyahi officer of Yazeed's army; he intercepted Imam from entering Kufa; changed sides; (he was the second to go to battle field)	from Kufa
65	Abu Thumama al-Saidi was at Battles of Jamal, Siffin, Nahrawan; expert horse-rider	from Kufa

Shielding the Imam

66	Saeed Abdullah al-Hanafi shielding Imam in prayers	from Kufa
67	Zuhayr Qayn commander of Imam's unit; shielding Imam in prayers; joined Imam at Zarud	from Kufa

Afternoon

68	Salman Muzarib Qays al-Bajali cousin of Zuhayr Qayn (Martyr 67)	from Kufa
69	Amr Qaraza Kab al-Ansari	from Kufa
70	Nafi Hilal al-Jamali was at Battles of Jamal, Siffin, Nahrawan	from Kufa
71	Shawdhab Abdullah joined Imam at Makkah	from Kufa
72	Abis Abi Shabib al-Shakhri	from Kufa
73	Abdullah Urwa	from Kufa
74	Abd Rahman Urwa (Martyrs 73 & 74 were brothers)	from Kufa
75	Hanzala Asad al-Shaybani	from Kufa
76	Saif Harith Sari Jabir al-Hamdani	
77	Malik Abd Sari Jabir al-Hamadani (Martyrs 76 & 77 were cousins)	
78	Jaun Ethiopian; helper of Imam Ali, Imam Hasan, Imam Husein	from Madinah
79	Wazeh Turkish; Imam's helper	from Madinah
80	Anas Harith al-Asadi companion of Prophet	from Madinah
81	Hajjad Masruq al-Jufi companion of Imam Ali; joined Imam at Makkah	from Kufa
82	Ziyad Arib al-Hamdani	
83	Salim Amr Abdullah	from Kufa
84	Saad Harith	from Madinah

85	Umar Jundab al-Hadrami was at Battles of Jamal, Siffin	from Kufa
86	Qanab Amr al-Numari	from Basra
87	Yazeed Nubayt al-Abdi joined Imam at Makkah; (father of Martyrs 33 & 34)	from Basra
88	Yazeed Mughfil al-Jufi was at Battle of Siffin	from Kufa
89	Rafi Abdullah	from Kufa
90	Bishr Amr al-Hadrami al-Kindi	from Kufa
91	Suwayd Abi Mata al-Khathami	

Martyrs from Abu Talib's Family

92	Abdullah Muslim Aqil Imam's cousin and nephew; Aqil's family	from Madinah
93	Muhammad Muslim Aqil Imam's cousin and nephew; Aqil's family	from Madinah
94	Jaffer Aqil Abu Talib Imam's cousin; Aqil's family	from Madinah
95	Abd Rahman Aqil Abu Talib Imam's cousin; Aqil's family	from Madinah
96	Abdullah Aqil Abu Talib Imam's cousin; Aqil's family	from Madinah
97	Muhammad Saeed Aqil Imam's cousin; Aqil's family	from Madinah
98	Muhammad Abdullah Jaffer Imam's nephew; Bibi Zainab's son; Jaffer's family	from Madinah
99	Aun Abdullah Jaffer Imam's nephew; Bibi Zainab's son; Jaffer's family	from Madinah
100	Qasim Hasan Ali Abu Talib Imam's nephew; Imam Hasan's (as) son	from Madinah

101 Ahmed Hasan Ali Abu Talib — from Madinah
Imam's nephew; Imam Hasan's (as) son

102 Muhammad Ali Abu Talib — from Madinah
Imam's brother; mother: Laila

103 Othman Ali Abu Talib — from Madinah
Imam's brother; mother: Ummul Baneen

104 Jaffer Ali Abu Talib — from Madinah
Imam's brother; mother: Ummul Baneen

105 Abdullah Ali Abu Talib — from Madinah
Imam's brother; mother: Ummul Baneen

106 Abbas Ali Abu Talib — from Madinah
Imam's brother; mother: Ummul Baneen;
Imam's standard-bearer at Karbala

107 Ali Akbar Husein — from Madinah
Imam's son; mother: Laila

108 Ali Asghar Husein — from Madinah
Imam's six month old son; mother: Rubab

109 Abdullah Hasan — from Madinah
Imam's nephew; Imam Hasan's (as) son

110 IMAM HUSEIN (as) — from Madinah

10 After Karbala

In this chapter, we will look at what happens to the survivors of Karbala, the effect the tragedy of Karbala has in the region and how it changes the political power of the rulers. We will also analyse as to who won this battle.

10.1 After Ashura day

- On 11 Muharram, the day after Ashura, Umar Saad and his soldiers bury their dead.

- The bodies of Imam Husein (as), his family and his supporters, many beheaded, are lying unburied in the desert of Karbala under the open sky.

- When Umar Saad has finished burying his people, he and his soldiers prepare to leave for Kufa.

- The only adult male to survive the tragedy is Imam Husein's (as) eldest son, Ali Zainul Abedeen; he is now the fourth Imam.

- Umar Saad orders all the survivors, except for Imam Ali Zainul Abedeen (as), should be tied with ropes and put on camels without any saddles so as to cause them the maximum discomfort during the journey to Kufa.

- Imam Ali Zainul Abedeen (as) is chained around his feet and hands, and an iron collar with inward spikes is put around his neck and is made to walk all the way to Kufa.

- In yet another act of cruelty in Karbala, the survivors who are now captives are made to pass through the battlefield where their family members are lying beheaded and unburied.

- The caravan of Umar Saad and the survivors leave Karbala in the afternoon and arrive at the outskirts of Kufa at night.

- Ubaydullah, the governor of Kufa, sends the message that they must spend the night there as he wants to stage-manage the entry as a victory parade, witnessed and celebrated by the locals in the daylight.

- Meanwhile, Khooli who brought the head of Imam Husein (as) from Karbala and kept it at his home at night brings it to Ubaydullah in the governor's palace on the morning of 11 Muharram.

- Ubaydullah orders that Imam Husein's (as) head should be sent to the outskirts of Kufa where the army and the survivors are gathered.

- On the day of Ashura in the afternoon, the heads of the seventy two martyrs were given to some officers to take to Kufa.

- What is known is that the heads of these seventy two martyrs formed part of the parade in Kufa.

- What is not known is whether on arrival at the outskirts of Kufa, they remained there for the night or were first taken to Ubaydullah and then brought back.

- By the evening of 11 Muharram, assembled on the outskirts of Kufa are the army of Umar Saad, the captives - the survivors of Imam Husein's (as) household - and the severed heads of Imam Husein (as) and the seventy two martyrs.

- The people of Kufa are told that a group of people who rebelled against the government of Yazeed have been killed and their women and children will be paraded through the streets in the morning.

10.2 Parade and captivity in Kufa

- It is the morning of 12 Muharram.
- The parade starts from the outskirts of Kufa through the streets and proceeding to the governor's palace.
- At the front are the heads of the martyrs mounted on spears; the captives - the survivors of the household of Imam Husein (as) - follow; they are bound by ropes, Imam Ali Zainul Abedeen (as) is still chained, the ladies are bareheaded with no scarf or veil.
- The soldiers are beating their drums and waving the flags in a show of victory.
- People are cheering the soldiers and jeering the captives.
- As the parade makes it way through the streets, some women ask the captives about their identity; when they find out that they are from the Prophet's Household, they are shocked, for they have been misinformed that the captives are some ordinary people who rebelled against the government of Yazeed.
- The ladies of Imam Husein's (as) family now begin their mission as present-day journalists and reporters.

- As we discussed in Section 5.5, Imam Husein (as) was determined to take the ladies with him, despite the advice from many people, precisely for this propose - for the truth to be told about what exactly happened at Karbala, and to counter any distortion or propaganda from the government controlled media in Kufa and Damascus.

- Thus, Lady Zainab and Lady Umme Kulthum, the sisters of Imam Husein (as) (see Chart 1 on the inside back cover) and Imam Ali Zainul Abedeen (as) tell the people about how the massacre unfolded in Karbala and how the women were humiliated.

- The heads of the martyrs and the captives are now presented to Ubaydullah in his palace; he has invited the government officials, dignitaries and some members of the public to be present there.

- He disrespects the head of Imam Husein (as) by poking it with his stick.

- On seeing this, an elderly companion of the Prophet is so appalled that he rebukes Ubaydullah, knowing the danger he will put himself in.

- He tells Ubaydullah to take his stick away, for how often has he seen the Prophet kiss the face that Ubaydullah is now disrespecting.

- Ubaydullah taunts, insults and ridicules the captives; he is eloquently answered by Imam Ali Zainul Abedeen (as) and Lady Zainab.

- The captives are imprisoned in Kufa until orders are received from Yazeed in Damascus about their fate.

- The head of Imam Husein (as) is paraded through the streets of Kufa and is then hung on the door of the governor's palace for public display.

- Ubaydullah sends a message to the governor of Madinah to inform the people that Imam Husein (as) and his male family members have been killed in Karbala.

10.3 Burial of martyrs

- On the morning of 11 Muharram, Umar Saad orders that all the dead from his side should be buried before they were to leave for Kufa in the afternoon.

- All the martyrs from the side of Imam Husein (as) are left lying unburied in the open on the plains of Karbala.

- When the whole army of Umar Saad leaves Karbala the tribe of Banu Asad from the surrounding villages take courage to come to the battlefield.

- When they see the beheaded bodies, they are shocked.

- Literature mentions two versions as to who buries the martyrs.

- According to one version, the tribe of Banu Asad buries the martyrs; another version says that Imam Ali Zainul Abedeen (as), the son of Imam Husein (as), miraculously appears in Karbala, identifies each martyr and helps the tribe of Banu Asad to bury them.

- Also, there are two different dates about when the martyrs are buried; either on 12 Muharram or 13 Muharram.

10.4 Parade and captivity in Damascus

- There is no mention in the literature about the number of days the captives are held in Kufa.

- Yazeed's instructions are that the heads of the martyrs and the captives should be sent to Damascus.

- Ubaydullah first sends an advance party of some army officers who carry the heads of the martyrs to Damascus.

- Later the captives are sent to Damascus; ladies and children tied with ropes and made to sit on camels without saddles; Imam Ali Zainul Abedeen (as) is chained and an iron collar is put around his neck; they are guarded and escorted by soldiers and some army officers including Shimr Ziljawshan, the murderer of Imam Husein (as).

- The caravan moves quickly to catch up with the advance party.

- The caravan of the captives, led by the heads of the martyrs, passes through several villages and towns on its way to Damascus.

- At every stop, the ladies take the opportunity to tell the people as to what exactly transpired in Karbala.

- The soldiers face hostility from the people along the route as the news of the truth of the tragedy of Karbala filters out.

- The caravan is made to take the indirect and longer route from Kufa to Damascus, rather than the shorter and more direct route; this is done to avoid ambushes from people who may have wanted to set the captives free (especially after seeing the sympathetic reaction of the people in Kufa when they realised that the captives are members of the Prophet's Household).

- The time taken for the journey from Kufa to Damascus is not mentioned in the literature; however, there are two accounts of the date of arrival in Damascus; in some literature, a date of 1 Saffar 61 AH (end October 680 AD), and in others, a date of mid-Rabil Awwal (mid December 680 AD) is given.

- The captives are made to wait for three days outside one of the gates of Yazeed's palace (present-day Umayyad Mosque) while the streets in the city are decorated; crowds come here to jeer and taunt the captives throughout this period.

- The streets of Damascus are decorated with ornaments, silk and colourful flags; drums are played in celebrations; people look their best; the whole city is in a festive and carnival mood; people are told this is to celebrate the victory of Yazeed over the defeat of the "rebels".

- Finally, after three days of waiting, the parade is now led through the crowded street to Yazeed's palace; at the front of the parade is the head of Imam Husein (as) followed by the heads of the other martyrs, and the captives; the captives are jeered all the way in.

- Inside the palace, Yazeed has gathered his government ministers, dignitaries, ambassadors and some members of the public.
- The head of Imam Husein (as) and of the other martyrs, and the captives in chains are brought before Yazeed.
- Like Ubaydullah, Yazeed disrespects the head of Imam Husein (as) by striking the lips with a stick and taunts, insults and ridicules Imam Ali Zainul Abedeen (as) and the ladies.
- Lady Zainab and Imam Ali Zainul Abedeen (as) publicly shame him and they answer to the taunts of Yazeed by giving eloquent sermons which are powerful, forceful, insightful and masterful.
- On hearing these sermons, the mood of the people in the hall changes from one of victory to shame, and they are now beginning to turn against Yazeed.
- Yazeed orders the imprisonment of the captives; they are put in a room of an old building without a roof where they are exposed to the heat of the day and the cold of

the night; they are also subjected to food rationing.

- He also orders that the heads of the martyrs are put on public display; they are hung on the palace gate for three days.

10.5 Coming home

- The captives are in Damascus for about one year.
- While in captivity, Sukaina, who is about five years old, the daughter of Imam Husein (as) (see Chart 1 on the inside back cover), dies in captivity and is buried in the prison.
- The ladies in Damascus visit the captives and they come to know about the atrocities in Karbala and how cruelly the captives have been treated since then.
- These ladies put pressure on their men and they in turn put pressure on Yazeed to set the captives free and to allow them to go back to their homes in Madinah.
- Yazeed is coming under increasing public pressure to set the captives free; so after

about one year in captivity, Yazeed sets them free.

- The captives request for a place where they can mourn and remember their dead family members, for until now, they get beaten by the guards whenever they mourn; a house is allocated to them and they mourn freely for seven days.

- This marks the birth of the institution of "majalis" gathering as we know it today, where people gather to mourn the tragedy of Karbala.

- Noman Bashir (who was the governor of Kufa when Muslim Aqil was rallying support for Imam Husein (as)), is given the task to ensure that the captives are safely escorted back to Madinah.

- The heads of the martyrs are also given back to them.

- On their way to Madinah, they make a detour to Karbala and arrive there on 20 Saffar 62 AH (November 681 AD), one year and forty days after the day of Ashura.

- The heads of the martyrs are buried in their graves.

- There is mourning and lamenting over the graves of the martyrs by the family members of Imam Husein (as), and after three days they leave for Madinah.

- Imam Ali Zainul Abedeen (as) stops the caravan just on the outskirts of Madinah; he sends a poet, Bashir Jazlam, to announce their arrival to the people of Madinah who come out to visit the survivors of Karbala.

- The caravan then enters Madinah and their first stop is at the Prophet's grave where they relate their trials and tribulations.

- The survivors of Karbala are back home after about one and a half years.

- The people of Madinah come to visit the family of Imam Husein (as) to offer their condolences; Imam Ali Zainul Abedeen (as) and the ladies tell them what happened in Karbala, and how Imam Husein (as), his family and his companions were brutally and mercilessly killed; they also relate about their sufferings when they were in captivity.

10.6 Madinah reacts

- The people of Madinah are shocked, angered and saddened when they hear about what happened in Karbala.

- They feel bad that they somehow allowed this to happen and did not give their support to Imam Husein (as).

- They are asking themselves how is it they have not realised the un-Islamic conduct of Yazeed and are beginning to realise why Imam Husein (as) decided to sacrifice his all to expose the regime of Yazeed and awaken conscience of the Muslims.

- They set up a commission of inquiry consisting of the elders of Madinah to investigate and report on the conduct of Yazeed.

- The commission is at pains not to include any member of the Hashimis (the Prophet's family) and the Umayyas (Yazeed's family) or anyone connected with the government in Madinah.

- This commission of inquiry is headed by Abdullah Hanzalah, and they go to Damascus.

- Yazeed is anxious that the commission reports favourably on him for Madinah's opinion is crucial to his credibility, especially now that even people in Syria are questioning his role in

Karbala and an opposition is building up against him.

- He offers all kinds of bribery to the commission, but the commission turns them down.
- When the commission returns to Madinah, they give a damning report on the character of Yazeed and his government.
- They ask the citizens of Madinah as to how it came about they were blind to all this and have failed to support Imam Husein (as) in his mission.
- The people of Madinah are so angry and disgusted that they chase out of Madinah about one thousand people who are connected with and supported Yazeed, including the current governor installed by him, Othman Muhammad Abu Sufyan (his nephew) and Marwan Hakam, the former governor.
- Abdullah Hanzalah, the head of the commission, takes over as the governor of Madinah.

10.7 Yazeed replies

- Meanwhile, seeing the success of Madinah in throwing out Yazeed's governor, Abdallah Zobayr in Makkah also declares himself independent of Syria and he installs himself as the governor of Makkah.

- Yazeed in Damascus is furious over the loss of two very important cities in his empire, Madinah and Makkah; so he sends an army of about twelve thousand soldiers to bring them back under his control.

- It is headed by Muslim Aqba and his deputy is Haseen Nameer (one of the army officer who was in Karbala).

- They are given a free hand to take any measure they want to recapture Madinah and Makkah.

- The only restriction is that the family of the Prophet's Household should not be touched or harassed, for Yazeed does not want any further backlash than the one he has to contend with at present; it is his own actions against the Prophet's Household that has resulted in the present crisis.

- Muslim Aqba leads the army into Madinah towards the end of Zilhaj 63 AH (end of August 683 AD).

- The two armies of Yazeed and Madinah meet at a place called Harrah, on the outskirts of Madinah; a fierce battle takes place and the army of Madinah is defeated; the army of Yazeed now advances towards Madinah.

- There follows three days of rampage, carnage and lootage in Madinah by the army of Yazeed; it is a free for all situation for the soldiers to do as they wish; many citizens of Madinah are killed and their properties looted.

- Even the Prophet's mosque is not spared of its sanctity; it is used as a stable for the horses; dogs are sat on the Prophet's pulpit and allowed to foul it; wine is drunk within the mosque.

- People who come to seek shelter in the Prophet's mosque are killed and the women are raped; about one thousand illegitimate children born as a result of the rapes by the soldiers of Yazeed.

- Muslim Aqba and the army stay in Madinah for about two months to consolidate their power and appoints a new governor.

- Towards the end of Muharram 64 AH (end of September 683 AD), the army leaves Madinah for Makkah to remove Abdullah Zobayr as a governor and bring Makkah under the control of Yazeed.

- In Makkah, Abdullah Zobayr receives the news of how Yazeed's army has terrorised the people of Madinah and it is now advancing to Makkah; he mobilises his army.

- On the way to Makkah, Muslim Aqba dies and the command shifts to Haseen Nameer.

- The two armies meet on the outskirts ok Makkah and are engaged in a battle for about a month; the forces of Abdullah Zobayr are trying to stop the advance of Haseen Nameer's army on the city.

- By early Rabil Awwal 64 AH (end October 683 AD), Haseen Nameer's troops are closing in around Makkah; they throw projectiles of burning pieces of wood on to the Kabah and it burns.

- For almost a month, while the fighting between the two armies continues, the Kabah remains burning.

- News suddenly reaches Haseen Nameer that Yazeed died in Damascus on 14 Rabil Awwal 64 AH (November 683 AD), three years after the tragedy of Karbala; he orders his soldiers to stop fighting and they return to Damascus.

10.8 The fall of Umayyas

We will list chronologically and give a brief description of the significant events which trigger the decline of the Umayyas as a result of the tragedy of Karbala.

61 – 62 AH (680 – 681 AD)

- The beginning of the downfall starts just two days after the day of Ashura, when Ubaydullah Ziyad in Kufa disrespects the head of Imam Husein (as) and he is rebuked by an elderly companion of the Prophet; such a challenge to the governor was unheard of before the tragedy of Karbala.

- Yazeed is similarly challenged in Damascus when he taunts and ridicules the family of Imam Husein (as); again, such a challenge to Yazeed was unthinkable before the tragedy of Karbala.

- Afraid of the backlash from the people Yazeed releases the captives from the prison in Damascus; yet another sign of the dwindling power of the Umayyas.

62 – 64 AH (680 – 683 AD)

- The home coming of the survivors to Madinah provides a catalyst for the people to investigate the true character of Yazeed
- This leads the people of Madinah and Makkah to break away from the control of Yazeed.

64 – 67 AH (683 - 687 AD)

- The death of Yazeed sparks off a rebellion against his governors in the cities of Madinah, Makkah, Kufa and Basra.
- Ubaydullah Ziyad is in Basra when the news of Yazeed's death comes in and when the rebellion breaks out, he escapes to Damascus.
- In Makkah, Abdullah Zobayr regains his control as governor and sends his men to Madinah and Basra to replace the Umayya appointed governors.
- The rebellion in Kufa forces the prison to be thrown open and all prisoners are released; Ubaydullah had imprisoned many supporters of Imam Husein (as), about four thousand, when Muslim Aqil was rallying support for him.
- They regroup to form a movement called the Tawwabun (The Penitents - people who feel sorry); they feel guilty that having invited Imam Husein (as) to Kufa, they were unable

(for most of them were imprisoned) to help him in his hour of need.

- Their primary mission is to go after Ubaydullah Ziyad who they hold responsible for the massacre at Karbala, and avenge the death of Imam Husein (as).

- Marwan Hakam, the Umayya leader in Damascus, mobilises an army under the command of Ubaydullah Ziyad to face the Penitents; in 65 AH (684 AD), they meet at Ayn al Warda, about half way between Damascus and Kufa; the Penitents suffer a crushing defeat; many of its members and leaders are killed and they retreat back to Kufa.

- Simultaneously, Mukhtar Thaqafee (who first hosted Muslim Aqil) in Kufa forms a parallel movement to avenge the killers of Karbala.

- Mukhtar's plan is to go after the officers and soldiers first and then aim for Ubaydullah Ziyad who has the support of the Umayya leader; his strategy is first to install himself as the governor of Kufa and then use the office to bring the killers to justice.

- After a lot of struggle, Mukhtar becomes the governor of Kufa in 66 AH (685 AD); during the eighteen months that he holds this office, he manages to round up about eighteen thousand perpetrators of Karbala and bring them to justice.

- Mukhtar is assassinated in 67 AH (687 AD) in a battle with an alliance of the armies of Makkah and Basra who want to control Kufa.

122 AH (740 AD)

- Imam Ali Zainul Abedeen (as) and the next two Imams after him keep away from the political movements that try to overthrow the Umayyas from power under the guise of avenging the tragedy of Karbala to gain political office.

- The movements of the Penitents and Mukhtar Thaqafee during the time of Imam Ali Zainul Abedeen (as) had no political motive at all.

- One of the sons of Imam Ali Zainul Abedeen (as) is Zayd; some people regarded him as the fifth Imam instead of Imam Muhammad Baqir (as).

- He leads the next major uprising against the Umayyas with the aim of avenging the killers of Karbala, against the advice of his nephew, Imam Jaffer Sadiq (as), the sixth Imam.

- In 122 AH (740 AD), he engages in a battle against the Umayyas; he and his supporters are heavily defeated and he is killed.

132 AH (749 AD)

- Amongst the sons of Abdul Mutallib are Abdullah and Abbas (see Chart 9 on page 265); Abdullah is the father of the Prophet.

- The descendants of Abbas (the Abbasis) are Hashimis and are related to the Prophet.

- Muhammad, a great grand-son of Abbas, forms a movement with the aim of overthrowing the Umayyas and rise to political power; he uses the guise of avenging the blood of Imam Husein (as) to gain support from the people; on his death, his son Ibraheem takes over the leadership.

- The Abbasi movement gets a lot of support from the people; for they want to overthrow the government of the Umayyas and since the Abbasis are related to the family of the Prophet, they are considered as a legitimate party to avenge the killers of Imam Husein (as).

- They send Abu Muslim, one of their supporters, to Khurasan (present-day Mashhad in Iran) to rally support for them.

- In 132 AH (749 AD), with the help of Abu Muslim's men from Khurasan, Abdullah Abu al-Abbas (with the title of al-Saffah) becomes the new leader in Iraq; his army marches to

Damascus and overthrows the Umayya leader from power.

- The Umayya dynasty comes to an end, seventy one years after the day of Ashura.

- This transfer of power occurs in the time of Imam Jaffer Sadiq (as), the sixth Imam.

- For ease of reference and a complete picture, Chart 10 on page 267 shows a ladder of the period and names of the Muslim political rulers when they are in power, overlapping with the names and birth-death years of the twelve Imams from the Prophet's Household.

- Note that the first two leaders are not from the Umayyas and hence their names are shown in brackets.

- Once the Abbasis consolidate their power in the Muslim empire, their conduct is no better than the Umayyas in persecuting the Prophet's Household and their followers.

10.9 Who won?

A battle results in a defeat, victory or stalemate; so the question is: who won at Karbala? Let us analyse a few points to answer this question.

The battle

- Imam Husein (as) lost all his supporters, including his own male family members, adults and children alike; he was also killed.
- By sheer numbers of soldiers in Yazeed's army, this battle was one sided as far as physical fighting was concerned.
- So the battle is lost by Imam Husein (as) militarily.
- However, as we shall see below Imam Husein (as) achieved victory in defeat.

Purpose of the battle

- Imam Husein's (as) stand all along was that he will never pledge his allegiance to Yazeed in order to ensure the survival of the Islamic ways.
- So the government cornered him, and then intimidated him by surrounding him and his supporters with a huge army.
- They even denied water to him and his family.

- They mercilessly and brutally killed every one of his male supporters, and did not even spare his six month old baby.

- Yet, despite all these atrocities, Imam Husein (as) still did not pledge allegiance to Yazeed.

- Such is the victory Imam Husein (as) that it has left an everlasting mark on the political scene, then and now.

- After the tragedy of Karbala, no succeeding political leader has dared to ask for a personal allegiance from any of the Imams of the Prophet's Household; they knew that they would never get it, even if it came to the point of death.

- Until now, no political leader of a country has dared ask for a personal allegiance or an endorsement for a government policy or action from the great religious scholars of the country.

- So, who has won? Undoubtedly, Imam Husein (as) has won.

Protests and challenges

- Before the tragedy of Karbala, no one, whether a private citizen, a government official or an ambassador could risk to protest or challenge the leader or the government of the time.

- After the tragedy of Karbala, such challenges and protests were now possible; in fact, Ubaydullah Ziyad in Kufa and Yazeed in Damascus were challenged by the people in their own palaces.

- They led to the beginning of the downfall of the Umayyas.

- So, who has won? Unquestionably, Imam Husein (as) has won.

Survival of Islamic ways

- Yazeed was not a suitable person to be the leader of the Muslims; this was agreed by all, including his own supporters.

- With Yazeed as the leader of the Muslims, Islamic ways and practices were in imminent and real danger of being distorted, corrupted and obliterated.

- Imam Husein's (as) primary mission was to save, at all costs, the Islamic ways and practices.

- It is the tragedy of Karbala that saved Islam from being vanquished, crushed and destroyed.

- People today have a choice to live an Islamic way of life or not; had it not been for Karbala, this choice would not be available for there would have been no Islam left.

- So, who has won? Unambiguously, Imam Husein (as) has won.

Role model

- Yazeed is notoriously remembered for flouting openly a decent and Islamic way of life, killing the Prophet's Household, looting the people of Madinah, desecrating the Prophet's mosque and burning the Kabah.

- Imam Husein (as) is lovingly remembered as a role model for standing up against corruption, oppression, falsehood and injustice; he achieves this by a supreme sacrifice for no personal motive or gain.

- So, who has won? Unequivocally, Imam Husein (as) has won.

Shrine

- It is said that where Yazeed is buried in Damascus is now a rubbish dump.
- None pays a visit to Yazeed's burial place.
- He is reduced to obscurity and is everlastingly reviled, hated and detested.
- In contrast, Imam Husein (as) is immortalised by building a shrine where he is buried in Karbala.
- Millions pay homage to Imam Husein (as) in Karbala.
- So, who has won? Unreservedly, Imam Husein (as) has won.

The flag of Imam Husein (as) might have fallen on the day of Ashura, but the spirit of the flag is flying high in every corner of the world for eternity.

References and Bibliography

A Chronology of Islamic History
H U Rahman, Ta-Ha, London, 1995
1-897940-32-7

A History of Medieval Islam
J J Saunders, Routledge, 1965

A Probe into the History of Ashura
Ibrahim Ayati, Islamic Seminary, Karachi, 1984

A Short History of the Arab Peoples
John Bagotglubb, Quartet Books, London, 1980
0-7043-3196-9

Alseart Selected Articles
Muhammadi Trust, London, 1983

Alseart The Imam Husayn Conference
Muhammadi Trust, London, 1986
0-7103-0207-X

Hazrat Muawiyah
Peermahomed Ebrahim Trust, Karachi, 1974

History of the Arabs
Philip K Hitti, Macmillan, Basingstoke, 1994
0-333-09871-4

History of the Caliphs
Rasul Jafarian (tr Ali Ebrahimi), Ansariyan, Qum, 2003
964-438-457-1

History of Islam (Volume 1)
Masudul Hasan, Adam, Delhi, 1992

Hossein (AS): A Warning and A Symbol
Jame Mosque; Tehran, 1980

Husain The Saviour of Islam
S V Mir Ahmed Ali, Ansariyan, Qum, 1991

Imam Husayn: The Savior of Islam
Compiled by Sayyid Muhammad Rizvi, Richmond, Canada, 1984

Imam Hasan and Caliphate
Qurrat-ul-Ain Abidiy (tr Sibtul Hasan Hansvi), Ansariyan, Qum, 2006
964-438-834-8

Imam Husayn and Tragic Saga of Karbala
Ali Nazari Munfared (tr Ali Ebrahimi), Ansariyan, Qum, 2001
964-438-277-3

Imam Hussein and The Day of Ashura
Al-Balagh Foundation, Tehran, 1992

Islamic History A New Interpretation I
M A Shaban, Cambridge University Press, Cambridge, 1990
0-521-29131-3

Islamic Shi'ite Encyclopaedia - Volume IV
Hassan Ul_Ameene, Beirut, 1973

Islam – Its Concepts and History
Mahmud-un-Nasir, Kitab Bhavan, Delhi, 1981

Karbala and Ashura
Ali Hussain Jalali, Ansariyan, Qum, 2002
964-438-374-5

Kerbala and Beyond
Yasin T al-Jibouri, Ansariyan, Qum, 1999
964-438-045-2

Kitab Al-Irshad – The Book of Guidance
Shaykh al-Mufid (tr Dr I K A Howard), Ansariyan, Qum

Kitab Maqtal al-Husayn
Abu Mikhnaf (tr Hamid Mavani), Canada, 2002

Lamentations Part II
M Ishtihardi (tr Arif Abdulhussain), Al-Mahdi Institute, 2001
1-902911-04-0

Lamentations Part III
M Ishtihardi (tr Arif Abdulhussain), Al-Mahdi Institute, 2005
1-902911-06-7

Misbah-uz-Zulam Roots of the Karbala Tragedy
Imdad Imam (tr Athar Husain Rizvi), Ansariyan, Qum, 2009
978-964-219-103-1

Mukhtar – How He Avenged The Kerbala Perpetrators
Mahmood Datoo, TTQ, New York, 2003
0-940368-34-X

Nafasul Mahmoom
Sheikh Abbas Qummi (tr Aejaz Ali Bhujwala), Ansariyan, Qum, 2005
964-438-654-X

Prophet Muhammad (saw) – A Concise Biography
Mahmood Datoo, Council of European Jamaats, London, 2008
978-0-9554035-4-5

Sulh al-Hasan
Radi al-Yasin (tr Jasim al-Rasheed), Ansariyan, Qum, 1998
964-438-014-2

The Apple of Sayyeda's Eyes
Peermahomed Ebrahim Trust, Karachi, 1973

The Biography of Amir Mukhtar
Peermahomed Ebrahim Trust, Karachi, 1973

The Caliphate
William Muir, Darf, London, 1984
1-85077-014-X

The Cambridge History of Islam (Volume 1A)
ed P M Holt et al, Cambridge University Press, Cambridge, 1992
0-521-29135-6

The Despotic Rulers
M J Mughniyyah (tr M Fazal Haq), Islamic Seminary, Karachi, 1985
0-941724-46-8

The Early History of Islam
Safdar Hosain, Peermahomed Ebrahim Trust, Karachi, 1983

The First Dynasty of Islam
G R Hawting, Routledge, Oxon, 2000
0-415-24073-5

The Heirs of the Prophet Muhammad
Barnaby Rogerson, Little Brown, London, 2006
0-316-72729-6

The Hidden Truth About Karbala
A K Ahmed, Ansariyan, Qum, 2007
978-964-438-921-4

The History of al-Tabari
Tabari, University of New York Press, USA:

Volume XV, The Crisis of the Early Caliphate, 1990	0-7914-0155-3
Volume XVI, The Community Divided, 1997	0-7914-2392-1
Volume XVII, The First Civil War, 1996	0-7914-2394-8
Volume XVIII, The Caliphate of Muawiyah, 1987	0-88706-314-4
Volume XIX, Caliphate of Yazid b Muawiyah, 1990	0-7914-0041-7
Volume XX, Collapse of Sufyanid Authority, 1989	0-88706-8567-X

The History of Islam
Akbar Shah Najeebabadi, Darussalam, Riyadh

Volume One, 2000	9960-892-87-5
Volume Two, 2001	9960-892-88-3

The History of Islam
Robert Payne, Barnes and Noble, New York, 1992
0-88029-562-7

The Life of Imam al-Hasan al-Mujtaba
Baqir Shareef al-Qurashi (tr Jasim al-Rasheed), Ansariyan, Qum, 2006
964-438-794-5

The Life of Imam Husain ('a)
Baqir Shareef al-Qurashi (tr Athar H S H Rizvi), Ansariyan, Qum, 2007
978-964-438-889-7

The Martyr For Mankind
Ali Naqi Naqvi (tr S Ali Akthar), Muhammadi Trust, London, 1986
0-946079-31-5

The Martyrdom of Husain
Abul Kalam Azad (tr Muhammad Iqbal Siddiqi), Noor, Delhi, 1985

The Mission of Imam Husain
Muhammad Yazdi (tr Ali Quli Qarai), Tehran, 1987

The Origins and Early Development of Shia Islam
S H M Jafri, Ansariyan, Qum, 1989

The Prophet and the Age of the Caliphates
Hugh Kennedy, Longman, London, 1986
0-582-19313-7

The Rising of al-Husayn
M M Shams al-Din (tr IKA Howard), Muhammadi Trust, London, 1985
0-7103-0191-X

The Role of Aishah in the History of Islam
Sayyid Murtadha Askari (tr A Pazargadi), Volume Three
Naba Organization, Tehran, 2000 964-6643-45-0

The Tragedy of Kerbala
Syed Mohsin Naquvi, Second ed, Mohsena, Princeton, 1992
0-961-727-3-0-6

The Umayyad Caliphate (65 - 86 AH)
Abd al-Ameer Abd Dixon, Luzac, London, 1971
7189-0149-5

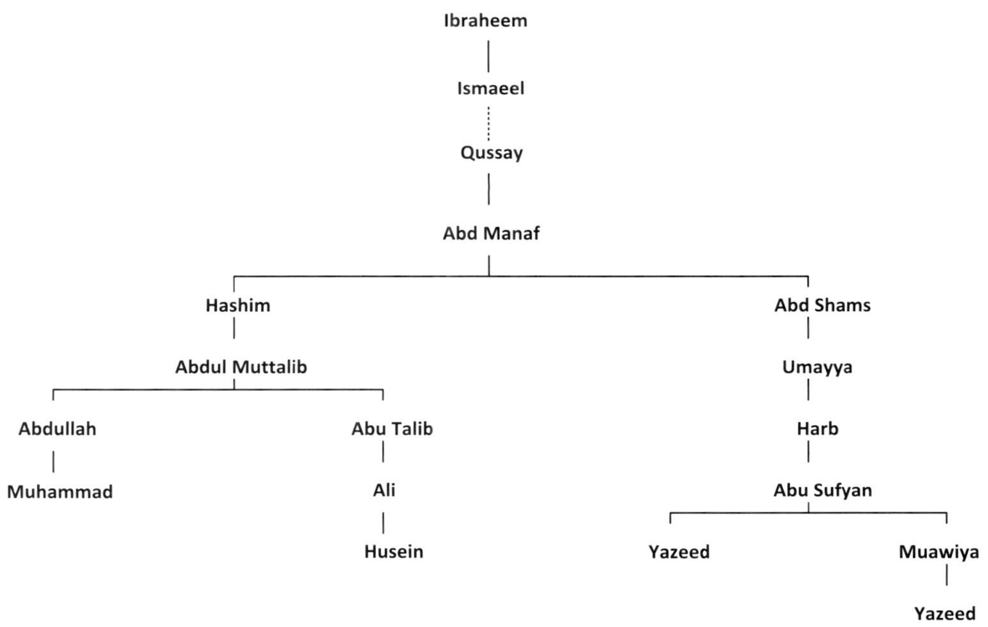

Chart 2
Ancestors of Imam Husein (as) and Yazeed

by Dr Mahmood Datoo

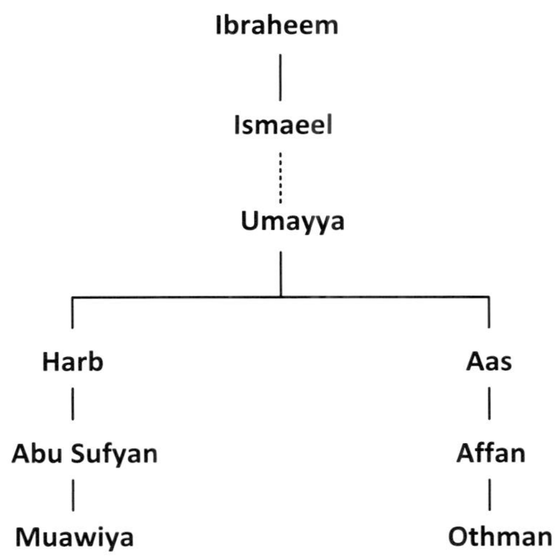

Chart 3

Muawiya - Othman Connection

by Dr Mahmood Datoo

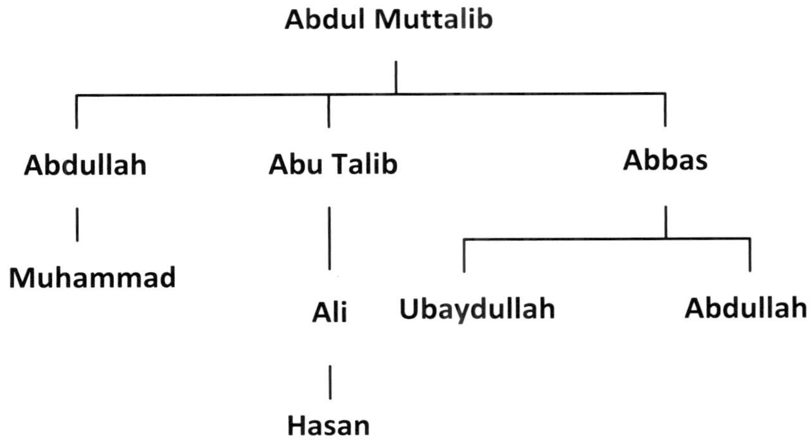

Chart 4

Imam Hasan (as) - Ubaydullah Connection

by Dr Mahmood Datoo

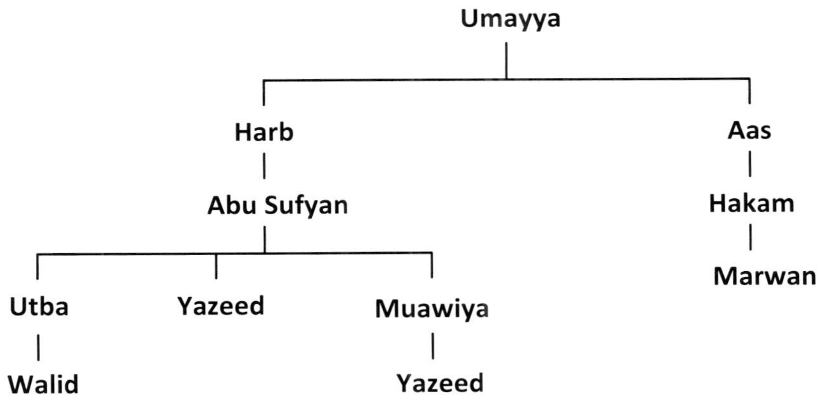

Chart 5

Yazeed - Walid - Marwan Connection

by Dr Mahmood Datoo

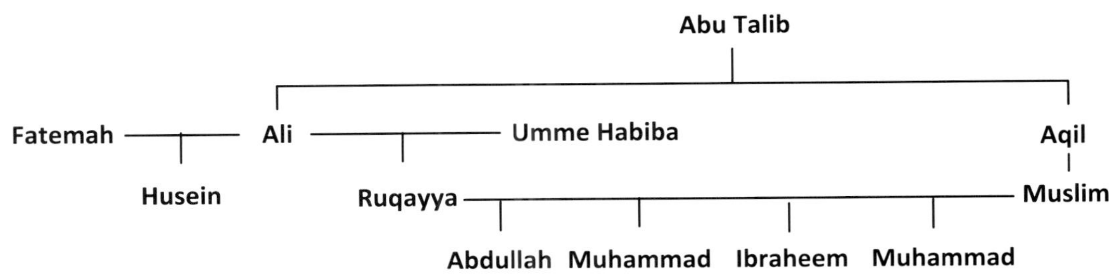

Chart 6

Imam Husein (as) - Muslim Aqil Connection

By Dr Mahmood Datoo

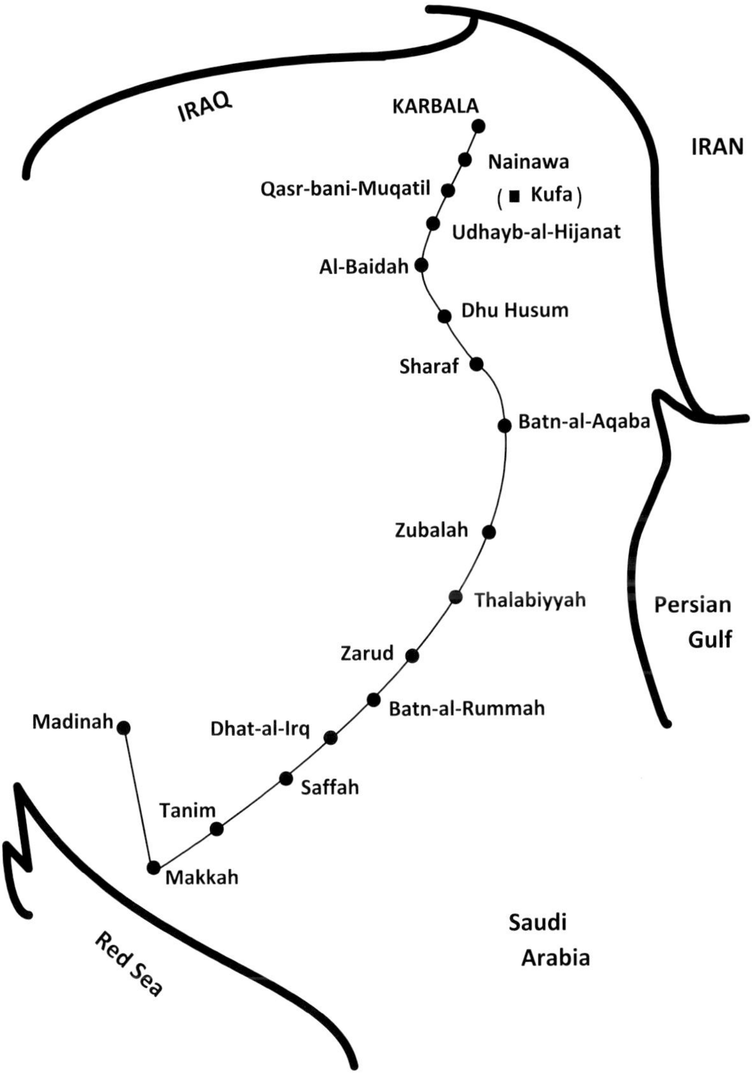

Chart 7
Makkah to Karbala
(not to scale)

by Dr Mahmood Datoo

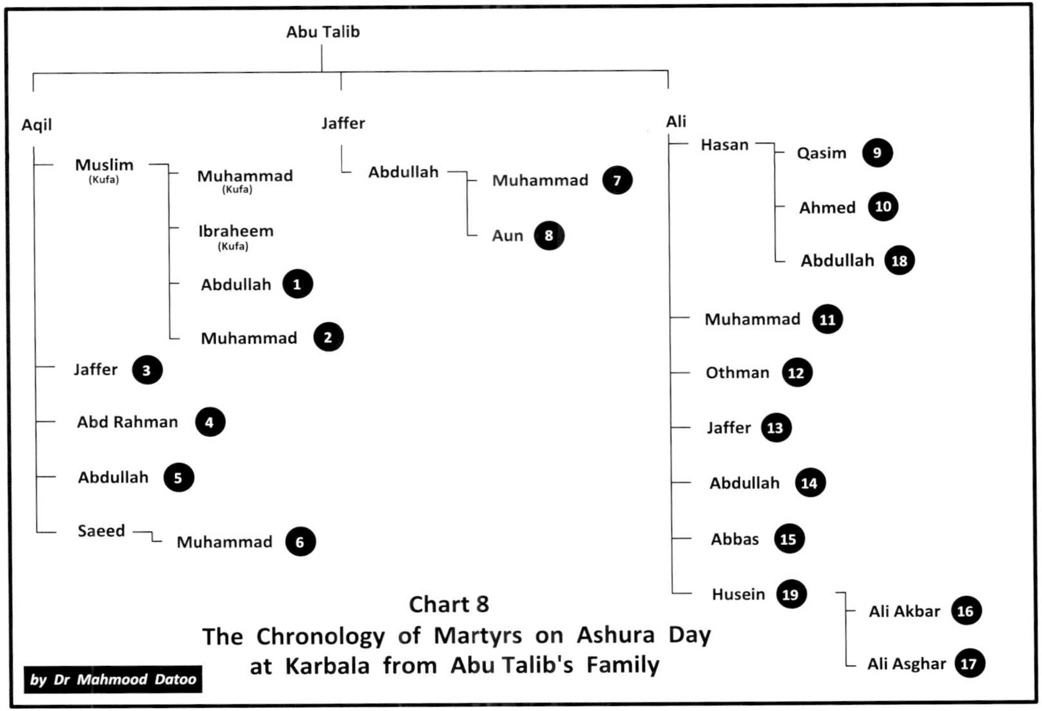

Chart 8
The Chronology of Martyrs on Ashura Day at Karbala from Abu Talib's Family

by Dr Mahmood Datoo

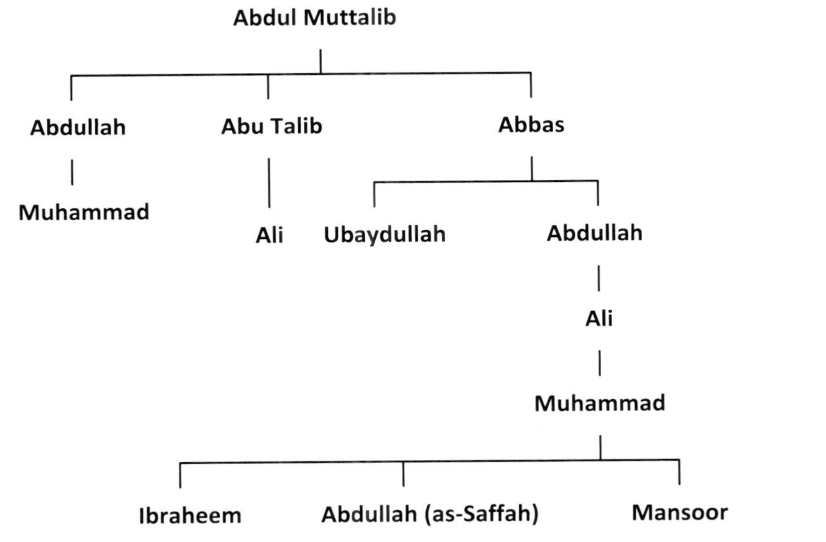

Chart 9
The Abbasis
(relevant parts only)

Chart 10

Time Ladder (in AH – Islamic Calendar)

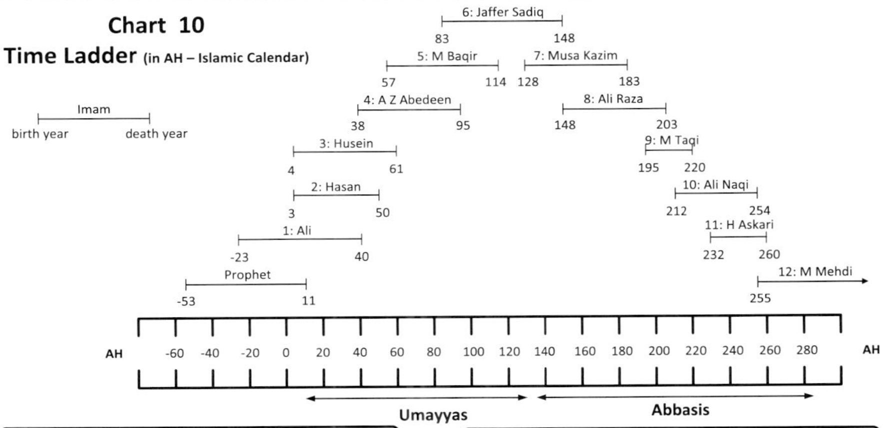

The Umayya Rulers

(Abu Bakr)	11 - 13	Sulayman	96 - 99
(Umar)	13 - 23	Umar	99 - 101
Othman	23 - 25	Yazeed	101 - 105
Muawiya	41 - 60	Hisham	105 - 125
Yazeed	60 - 64	Walid	125 - 126
Muawiya	64 - 64	Yazeed	126 - 126
Marwan	64 - 65	Ibraheem	126 - 127
Abdul Malik	65 - 86	Marwan	127 - 132
Walid	86 - 96		

The Abbasi Rulers

Abdullah	132 – 136	Wasiq	227 - 232
Mansoor	136 - 158	Mutawakkil	232 - 247
Mahdi	158 - 169	Muntasir	247 - 248
Musa	169 - 170	Mustayeen	248 - 252
Haroon	170 - 193	Motazz	252 - 255
Amin	193 - 198	Mohtadi	255 - 256
Mamoon	198 - 218	Motamad	256 - 279
Motasim	218 - 227		

by Dr Mahmood Datoo